T0193175

Love Changes Things

Even in the World of Politics

Caroline Cottom, PhD

iUniverse, Inc.
Bloomington

Love Changes Things
Even in the World of Politics

Copyright © 2012 Caroline Cottom, PhD

All rights reserved. No part of this book may be used or reproduced by
any means, graphic, electronic, or mechanical, including photocopying,
recording, taping or by any information storage retrieval system
without the written permission of the publisher except in the case
of brief quotations embodied in critical articles and reviews.

The author has used the real names of most U.S. and Soviet government
officials and leaders of nonprofit organizations. The names of a few
other individuals have been changed to protect their privacy.

iUniverse books may be ordered through booksellers or by contacting:

iUniverse
1663 Liberty Drive
Bloomington, IN 47403
www.iuniverse.com
1-800-Authors (1-800-288-4677)

Because of the dynamic nature of the Internet, any Web addresses or
links contained in this book may have changed since publication and
may no longer be valid. The views expressed in this work are solely those
of the author and do not necessarily reflect the views of the publisher,
and the publisher hereby disclaims any responsibility for them.

Any people depicted in stock imagery provided by Thinkstock are models,
and such images are being used for illustrative purposes only.

Certain stock imagery © Thinkstock.

ISBN: 978-1-4697-8106-8 (sc)
ISBN: 978-1-4697-8108-2 (hc)
ISBN: 978-1-4697-8107-5 (e)

Printed in the United States of America

iUniverse rev. date: 3/20/2012

I believe that unarmed truth
and unconditional love
will have the final word in reality.

Martin Luther King, Jr.

God alone knows the mind of a person,
and the duty of a man of God
is to act as he is directed by his inner voice.
I claim that I act accordingly.

Mohandas K. Gandhi

Contents

Preface

The United States of America conducted its last nuclear test explosion in September 1992. At the time, the United States and Russia had over 40,000 nuclear weapons between them. The U.S. government's decision to end nuclear testing was not made in a vacuum. Millions of people worldwide participated for several decades in urging an end to testing as a way to slow and reverse the nuclear arms race. In the U.S., a coalition of 75 national organizations, formed in the late 1980s, worked diligently toward this end.

Many factors led to this astounding victory. One factor, little known at the time, was the creation of loving relationships with persons in key decision-making roles. Without these relationships, testing would not have ended when it did.

Love Changes Things...Even in the World of Politics is my version of how this took place.

This story brings together two realms that many think are mutually exclusive: spirituality and politics. Indeed, there is typically a wide chasm between the two. In my story, they came together in a miraculous way and provided a crucial piece that enabled testing to stop.

People committed to political change may turn away from this story because they believe that spirituality is irrelevant to their work. Others, who have opened themselves to a spiritual life, may turn away because they do not wish to be involved in the business of politics. I am convinced that integrating the two is essential to our future, and that many of us are required to do this work.

Because of the personal nature of this story, my decision

to publish the book as nonfiction was not taken lightly. Our planet is in peril. I believe that reflecting on what happened here can help us understand the power of love to change things in places where decisions affect the lives of billions of people, animal life, and the fate of the planet herself.

Introduction: Finding Our Way Home

For much of my life I've had a strong sense of where I was to go and what I was to do, as though Hollywood had scripted my journey. I have felt like Dorothy, uprooted from Aunt Em's farm by a tornado, on my way to Oz with no idea what adventures I would encounter along the way. I was baffled why particular experiences fell in my lap, yet certain I was headed in the right direction.

I've often stood at the fork of diverging trails—one that led through a meadow that opened ahead of me, and another that disappeared into a tangled wood or a thick curtain of fog. The instructions were always firm and always clear: "No, you cannot go the easy way. You must venture into the unknown."

If I mustered my courage and walked tentatively into the fog, I would eventually find myself at the edge of a cliff. "I knew it!" I'd exclaim, as though I had caught the path itself in a punishing act. I'd been right to be scared. There was no trail down the escarpment. Nothing but a free fall between me and the shallows below.

At this point a not-very-gentle voice would kick in. "Don't mind me, sweetie, but your road ends here, and you've got no other choice, so jump."

Jump? And risk breaking my neck?

Each time, I held myself close and shivered, wondering why this particular thing—the hardest thing, it seemed at the time—was being asked of me. But in every case, if I pinched my nose and jumped off the cliff into the currents below, a life raft would materialize to cushion my fall.

It didn't matter that the raft later developed holes or became trapped in the rocks, spinning in circles until it broke free, because downstream were magical encounters and luminous lands I could never have imagined. Not in my wildest, most fantastic dreams.

I was grateful that many signs appeared along the way and that not all asked for such leaps of faith. The messages were always close at hand, like a sparrow twittering under the eaves, or the wind whispering in a stand of trees. Over time I learned that all I had to do was ask, then listen for answers.

I had majored in English literature at a small college north of Los Angeles, then taught high school English and special education for several years, including a stint with the Peace Corps in Thailand. After Southern California, my husband and I moved to Nashville, Tennessee, where I earned my doctorate in educational policy, then directed a board of local government. We lived in Tennessee for over a decade, becoming deeply involved in community life.

I awoke one day to find myself living in the nation's capital, heeding the messages of my dreams, talking to the voice of Spirit*, and working in the arena of international arms control. Suddenly, unexpectedly, I was rafting the waters of exotic jungles, from the halls of Congress and the federal bureaucracy, to the sparkling city of Reykjavik, Iceland, and the deserts of Kazakhstan. I found myself meeting with ambassadors and vice presidents, addressing delegates to the United Nations, and giving interviews on national and international TV, most of the time while feeling terrified and inadequate for the task.

Clues about where to go and what to do next often came in dreams or from an inner voice. If I slowed down enough to listen, I could hear exactly the truth I needed in a line of poetry, in words spoken by a minister from the pulpit, or in the wisdom of a friend. The messages told me to love the people I worked with—not in a romantic or physical way—but spiritually, unconditionally, without expectation of anything

---

*   I use "God" and "Spirit" interchangeably to refer to the creative, loving, omnipresent force that pervades everything.

in return. I took these messages to heart, allowing each one to direct and empower me along the way.

Everyone receives messages in this manner—it is how Spirit and the divine intelligence of the cosmos speak to us— but many do not listen, and fewer still act on what they hear. We are all capable of opening ourselves to learning on many levels. We learn not only through our intellect and our rational minds. We dream, we sense, and we feel with our hearts and bodies. Each of us can tune into the rhythms of nature, the deepest longings of a nation of people, or the innermost struggle of an elected official. We can hear and respond to the good intention behind someone else's, or our own, confusing behavior. Indeed, if we quiet our minds, we can hear the voice of Spirit calling us to a life of greater truth and meaning.

These insights accompanied me when I moved to Washington and became immersed in its political milieu. Each morning I crossed Capitol Hill along with hundreds of young, smartly dressed men and women on their way to jobs that would affect the future of the nation. Striding crisply, converging on congressional offices in droves, they carried attaché cases full of important papers that were written, condensed, and studied the night before.

Washington's political air is clear, bright, heady; the Capitol building, a focal point for all that humming activity. Walk to the building's west side, where the Mall spreads out before you, its own beautiful city. The Mall exudes a sense of order and calm in its layout, splendid greenery, and the architecture of its dozen museums. At its midpoint, the Washington Monument, in a circle of American flags, points to the heavens, focused and direct, determinedly masculine. Beyond, the long rectangular pool—feminine answer to the monument—receives images and reflects them skyward, mirroring the soul of America. Gravel paths meander in pleasant reverie, but one can always go back to the obelisk and gaze into the pool, in its reflection watch planes soar overhead as clouds billow and loft.

The Mall evidences an integration of art and history, science and nature, masculine and feminine, that political Washington lacks. In time I came to see the political machinery of Congress, the federal bureaus, and all the supporting agencies and associations as the "head" of our country; a bodiless, almost soulless, place where ideas are the currency of exchange. Human emotions, body, soul, and spirit—the realms of feeling, sensation, intuition, and dreams—have low credibility among most politicians, bureaucrats, and policy analysts. If I'd been working in any other part of the country, my spiritual experiences might have seemed strange; in D.C., they were unmentionable.

I began to see these other realms as Washington's shadow side: those aspects of life that are denied, ignored, or hidden from view. Surely politicians and arms control analysts go to church or temple, get inspiration from nature, and listen to their hearts, I thought. Surely they have flashes of insight and pay attention to their dreams. Or do they? I am certain that some do, but such experiences are given little credibility in Washington's political culture, so they are rarely recognized or shared.

As I looked for clues that the emotions-body-soul-spirit of life existed here too, I began to encourage those aspects in the leaders I met, hoping to help connect our country's head to its body, heart, and soul. In part, this meant connecting our leaders to the dreams and wishes of ordinary people all over the country. In part, it meant caring about the leaders themselves in a deep and special way.

This is the heart and soul of my story: loving and encouraging decision makers to value the totality of who they are. My work was to hold these people in the highest possible regard while staying as clear as I could about my message and my task. This meant honoring the spirit and loving intentions of each person, while maintaining integrity around my own values and goals.

And thus we return to Oz. On life's journey, each of us is Dorothy, tap dancing along in our glittery red shoes, surprised by all manner of events as we travel this golden highway. Along the way I discovered something very important: that each of us is also a wizard, capable of giving one another a body, a heart, or a soul. We can make a difference in other people's lives by caring about them, supporting their personal and spiritual growth, and encouraging them to take care of themselves.

Each soul is precious, each person's path worthy of our attention. Yet what better lives to affect than the lives of those who are running our country?

Book One: The Gift

One American.

Teacher, writer, workshop leader. Married, no children.

One American story. I had many good friends and many connections within my community, but I had never studied political science and had no experience in the realm of politics, with one exception:

In California in the early 1970s, Herb Lobell, director of a statewide association dedicated to serving the needs of handicapped children, picked me as his legislative director. I had no idea what the job entailed, but Herb took me under his wing, teaching me about legislation, lobbying, and legislative strategy. Under Herb's guidance, I wrote one piece of legislation and testified in one hearing—the extent of my political involvement. That one piece of legislation, granting services to handicapped children, was subsequently passed into law by the California State Legislature. It was an omen of things to come.

In the summer of 1983, I was recovering from my younger sister's death at the age of thirty-two, working as a community organizing consultant in rural Tennessee, and writing my sister's story.

Then I was struck by lightning.

1
Out of the Blue

June 17, 1983.

The day was sultry, hot. In the front yard, trees wilted and drooped. The sidewalks sizzled like water dripped over heated rock as insects hummed an undertone, the slow beating of wings flapping through soup.

It was my fifth day of house-sitting, on writing retreat. I paced Louise's dark living room, my sandals flopping across the brown swirl of high-low carpet. *What scene should go next? Does the ending for Chapter 5 work?* Overhead a fan clicked and whirred as an air conditioner thumped in the kitchen nearby, a poor effort against the oppressive heat. It sounded like the beating of dusty carpets: whap, whap.

I paused to stare at a straggly spider plant and pots of ivy nesting on the sill. Ten feet away, through smudged double windows, a white clapboard house glared in the midday sun. I wrinkled my nose at the smell of mildew and must and squinted at the white house, hands on my hips.

I was staring at the house when it struck: a surge of energy that fired my neck, with sparks shooting up and down my right arm. My neck took the brunt of the charge, pulsing with spasms of pain.

I grasped the side of my neck and moaned. "My god," I said aloud, shaking. "What was that?"

My mind fogged. Lightning? Electricity? It didn't make sense. I made my way to the couch and sat down, my thoughts scrambled. Still clenching my neck, I stared ahead at the brown walls, the orange framed prints from Korea, the carpet swirls. How to understand what just happened?

The physical pain was real, my muscles raw and sharp, my head pounding, yet the lightning bolt didn't seem to be a physical event. There was no electrical storm, no contact with electricity, no key on a kite. Was it a message from God, or another world? And what kind of message, for heaven's sake?

I searched my soul for the next two hours, trying to make sense of the experience. An answer came, which I quickly rejected. But the more I asked, the more it persisted. The same answer, over and over, more loudly each time, as though addressed to someone who was deaf.

"You are to build a relationship with Al Gore, Jr.," said a voice of authority. And the thought struck me with absolute terror.

When this zag of lightning appeared, it was lush and tropical outside, wet and hot as a rain forest, a typical Nashville summer. A tapestry of green wove itself up the sides of houses, mailboxes, and telephone poles, anything that stood still.

I was in my late thirties and happily ensconced with my husband and two cats in a brick bungalow about to be overrun with ivy. Ron worked for Avco Corporation, the cats lazed around on their backs, and I wrote chapters for a book about my sister, occasionally consulting for a nonprofit legal services group that served fifteen counties in rural Tennessee.

Two years earlier I had become involved in nuclear disarmament—the Nuclear Freeze movement of the early 1980s. In the winter of 1981, I had discovered that the United States and the Soviet Union had over 50,000 nuclear weapons between them. Astounded that I hadn't known this before, I began attending meetings of Nashville's newly formed Freeze group and read everything about the arms race I could find.

The following summer I joined a busload of Nashvillians in a nationwide caravan to New York City. On June 12, 1982, cheered by homeless people, policemen, and Wall Street bankers, we marched through the city to Central Park. The mood was electric; everyone was excited. At the park, organizers waved signs that read "One Million." One million people calling for an end to the nuclear arms race! The throngs of young men and women, gray-haired couples, and parents with strollers struck me with a force like nothing I could remember.

Conservative as a young adult and uninvolved politically, I had missed the civil rights movement. I had watched my college friends grieve at the loss of Martin Luther King, Jr., in a way I could not understand. It was Central Park that convinced me I didn't want to miss the disarmament movement, too. I returned to Nashville determined to do what I could.

Our Freeze group was fired up by the trip to New York. When asked to chair the group, I enthusiastically agreed. I led biweekly meetings and worked with the Freeze staff, Paul Slentz and Louise Morris, to develop a strategy that included meeting with our congressman, Bill Boner, and with Tennessee's shining star, Albert Gore, Jr., the congressman for a neighboring district.

Gore carried the family history and physical presence of a thoroughbred. The son of a former U.S. senator, he had jumped into a congressional race in the early 1970s to shouts of "Gore for President!" Tennesseans knew he was destined to lead the United States of America, so his election to Congress was a foregone conclusion.

The fact that Gore wasn't Nashville's congressman didn't matter when it came to estimating his importance to our cause. He planned to run for Senate the following year, certain to be elected by a wide margin, and he had begun to carve out a niche for himself in the field of nuclear arms control. He had made it clear this was going to be his issue.

By contrast, Bill Boner distanced himself from the very word "disarmament." Heeding the demands of major defense contractors in our district, Boner voted for every weapons system the Pentagon proposed, so we were not surprised when his office ignored our request for a meeting.

But Gore was interested, and early one Saturday morning

in February 1983, four members of Nashvillians for a Nuclear Arms Freeze braved icy streets to meet him in a dormitory lounge at Vanderbilt University.

We picked our way along slippery sidewalks, exhaling white vaporous puffs, and located an unlocked door at International House, then roamed the halls till we found the lounge. It was my job to let Gore know we had arrived. I was nervous dialing his room at the nearby Holiday Inn and surprised when his voice came on the line. I tried to sound relaxed, but my heart pounded and my stomach fluttered.

As the five of us sat in a dark-paneled room with the radiator spewing moist heat, I became intensely aware of my clothing: thick heavy wool, tweed vest over wool sweater, flannel skirt. I was unfamiliar with the territory, intimidated by the congressman's position of power, and bowled over by his earnest self-confidence. He was young and cowlicked, his face clear and untroubled, with an intense serious smile.

Throughout the meeting, he leaned forward, hands clasped between his knees, explaining his position and listening carefully to ours. When Paul presented the Freeze position, Gore talked about the dangers inherent in stopping all at once. But he said he was open to supporting a Freeze if it were in the form of a resolution. He mentioned a proposal before the House that would fund a missile called the Midgetman, a weapons system he thought might shift the focus on both sides of the Atlantic toward smaller weapons. He was interested in knowing how many people we were in contact with in Nashville and around the state. Despite our different views on strategy, we ended the meeting amicably and agreed to stay in touch.

I wrote a letter thanking him for his time, and over the next few months occasionally spoke with his staff about upcoming votes. We discussed two pieces of legislation: a resolution calling for a freeze on testing, building, and deploying nuclear weapons (the Nuclear Freeze Resolution); and an amendment to the Defense bill to fund the MX missile, a new ten-warhead nuclear weapons system, in which each missile was designed to fire ten nuclear warheads at once. His staff indicated he would vote for a freeze, but they were less than candid about his position on the MX. Our group was astonished when his pro-Freeze vote was followed immediately by a vote to fund the new weapons system. Worse, Gore had played a key role in assuring that the MX vote was successful, bargaining with the Reagan administration to keep alive the Midgetman, in exchange for Gore's support for the MX. Even though we knew Gore considered himself a "raging moderate," the disarmament group was incensed. We couldn't understand what was moderate about a multi-billion-dollar weapons system that could fire ten nuclear warheads at once.

The fact that Gore, who seemed so intelligent and educated on arms control issues, could flip-flop in such a manner baffled us. Our meeting at Vanderbilt had left a strong positive impression. He had seemed genuine and sincere, the furthest thing from an opportunist. It appeared that we were wrong about him, that maybe everyone was wrong.

After my lightning bolt experience, and from the vantage point of my writing retreat, I knew it was important for our local group to stay in touch with the congressman. I could see that my having a cordial relationship with him would be helpful, especially since everyone else in the group was disgusted with him and refused to write or call his office.

I did not feel confident to handle the nuances of a relationship with a member of Congress. Nor was I convinced that he would be open to such a prospect, given my perception that members of Congress chose to insulate themselves from most of their constituents.

Nevertheless, my neck continued to throb as though gripped with a steel clamp, and the idea that I should build a relationship with Gore stalked me like a wolf, breathing over my shoulder when I sat down to write, ate lunch, and lay down at night to sleep. It became nearly impossible to focus on writing the book about my sister, and finally I gave in. It seemed I had no choice but to follow the message I'd been given.

To allay my anxiety, I promised myself I would commit to one small, manageable task: I would write Gore once a month in the hope that I might eventually get through to him with my ideas about the nuclear arms race. In my grander moments, I thought that I might even influence his thinking, but mostly I dreaded entering the political arena at all.

I sat down at Louise's kitchen table to draft a letter, pencil and yellow pad in front of me, a glass of iced tea sweating circles on the beige-speckled Formica top. I doodled and made notes, but in the back of my mind the outline of another table took shape, an image from a recent dream:

It is tea time; a round, white table is set with spoons and cups. The air wafts gently, a perfect kind of day. Albert Gore, Jr., and I are at an outdoor café, sipping tea as we talk. Around us are potted geraniums, splotches of fuchsia and pink. He had said, "I will give you an hour," and this was our appointed time.

Many people try to interrupt us. He deals with them briefly while focusing his attention on me. Then a woman approaches holding a male infant in her arms and a small girl by the hand. She says she needs to speak with him. He and I continue to talk, but he gives her his attention, too, as she sits down near our table.

The woman and her baby exude the serenity of a painting by Raphael. The girl stands very close, and all three are held in a sacred light. All is nurturing as well; the woman seems like an ancient Earth goddess. Al Gore watches the woman earnestly, as though seeing what he can learn from her, and I am amazed by his attentiveness.

When the dream came to me earlier in the week, its sensual quality had grabbed my attention. Feminine images were abundant: the mother and baby, her girl child, the round table with spoons and cups, pink and fuchsia flowers, paintings by Raphael, and an ancient Earth goddess. I had written down the dream, studied it, and given it a title: "He Listens to Women in Order to Learn." I thought this was the core message of the dream, him listening and observing the feminine.

I was familiar with the concept that all parts of a dream are aspects or reflections of one's self. Thought of in this way, Gore might represent an inner masculine aspect of myself that was becoming more competent at handling things out in the world, what Swiss psychiatrist Carl Jung called the *animus*. If this were true, then perhaps my fear about building a relationship with Gore was associated with this: Building a relationship might accompany coming into my own power.

I also wondered if the dream were telling me something about Gore himself. Was he becoming more attuned to the feminine, to those aspects of himself that were nurturing, intuitive, receptive? I had been impressed with the way he listened to us at Vanderbilt. Was the dream telling me something I needed to know about him, or was it merely reflecting what I had already observed?

Thinking about the dream helped me formulate what I wanted to say in my letter. I believed strongly that the roots of the arms race were in racism and sexism, in seeing people who are different from us as evil or threatening, and in ignoring the views of women as well as the feminine aspects of one's self. I knew that most people making decisions about nuclear weapons were Caucasian and male, so I decided to address this point in my letter, making the case for why he needed a female perspective.

I settled on three additional goals: to appreciate him for the things he'd done that our local group agreed with, to tell him about myself and my role in the statewide Freeze campaign, and to share my ideas about how we might work together to end the nuclear arms race. Then I wrote three pages.

That afternoon I walked to the mailbox through a world of stillness. The streets were empty, the trees motionless, the houses in retreat, shades drawn. At the corner, I paused for a moment, took a deep breath, then dropped the letter into the slot. I seemed to know I was in for a surprising ride. Never one to enjoy roller coasters, I wondered how I could safely buckle myself in.

Later, when I told a friend about my experience and the

decision to write Gore once a month, she laughed. "Hold onto your hat!" she said, a twinkle in her eyes.

I'll write once a month for three years, I promised myself when I drafted that first letter, thinking maybe I'd get through to him by then.

In fact, Gore's administrative assistant, the head of his Washington office, called me as soon as he got the letter.

"Who *are* you?" he asked, with a tone that suggested he thought I had dropped by parachute into left field.

"I chair the Nuclear Freeze group …," I began, but I realized that wasn't what he meant. He wanted to know why they hadn't known about me before.

Peter Knight called three times that week, and I was thrilled. It might take Al Gore three years to notice my letters, but apparently I'd gotten through to his administrative assistant on the first try. By the end of the week, he had arranged for Gore to visit our local group on his next trip to Middle Tennessee, at the end of July.

I reread my letter. It was not an ordinary constituent's letter. I had praised his clear thinking and his humanness and had asserted boldly that I was his female counterpart back home, in touch with his constituents on the issue we both cared so much about. And it was three pages. Lobbying manuals urge brevity. "Don't go beyond one page," they instruct, "or it will never be read."

I knew the risk, but I had decided on a different course because I wanted to reach beyond the formalities, beyond the walls that keep elected officials separated from everyone else. I had wanted to touch the person.

My decision was based on experience as a community organizer and an approach to social change I had developed over several years. It was grounded in human values: listening, treating others with respect, and searching for common ground. I had used these skills in Freeze meetings, at tables we'd set up at local fairs, and on door-to-door petition drives.

I had led workshops for social activists where I taught them how to do social change work "from the heart." Until recently, I had not thought to take these skills into the hardest places—the defense industry, the Pentagon, and the halls of Congress—the places of power.

Buoyed by Peter's response, I worked with Paul and Louise to plan the meeting with Rep. Gore. We decided to invite a core group of supporters with diversity of occupation, gender, and race. We pored over lists of activists and community leaders, finally selecting twenty people to whom we would send personal invitations.

At the meeting we would sit in a circle and introduce ourselves so that Gore knew who was there. We would ask him to present his position, then Paul would present ours, followed by a discussion that I would facilitate, striving for dialogue and communication. We hoped to get answers to our questions about Gore's approach to arms control policy, particularly his decision to support the MX missile. More importantly, we hoped to begin to establish a relationship of mutual trust and respect.

Meanwhile Gore wrote an op-ed for the *Washington Post* in which he acknowledged that the Freeze debate in Congress had challenged the foundations of the old thinking about nuclear weapons and the arms race. The Freeze folks had forced the experts to revisit the essence of the issue, he said—not how best to design imaginary scenarios for destroying the Soviets, but how best to save civilization from the horror of nuclear destruction. We felt it was a very good outcome of our beginning to work with Gore.

Several of us arrived early to set up the room: chairs in a circle, three at one end, and a table with Freeze literature, a coffee pot, and cookies baked by volunteers. As everyone gathered, we stood in clusters chatting, waiting for Gore. At twenty-five minutes past the hour, Gore arrived with a small entourage. "He's here!" someone whispered, and a hush fell over the room.

Paul met the congressman at the door, shook his hand, and greeted him loudly. The rest of us went back to talking, but we were aware of Gore's every move. He stood out in the crowd: a tall man with shiny black hair in a dark blue suit and red tie. He worked his way from person to person, shaking hands, introducing himself, often stopping to talk. I was impressed with the care that went into this process.

Finally he reached the group where I stood. I extended my hand and introduced myself, unsure if he would remember me from the Vanderbilt meeting five months earlier.

But he surprised me. He smiled in recognition, put his hand on my shoulder, and said warmly, sincerely, "Thank you for being my friend."

The Blue.

Out of the blue!

Out of the blue came a lightning bolt, my three-page letter to Gore (which was "out of the blue" for them), Peter's enthusiastic response, and Al Gore, Jr., thanking me for being his friend. Out of the blue, indeed.

And where is that "blue" from which such amazing things could happen? It was clearly not my ego, which was timid, anxious, and afraid. That "blue" dragged me into relationships with Gore and his administrative assistant "kicking and screaming," as they say.

No, the Blue was some divine instrument calling me to live boldly in a world that was a total mystery to me: the world of politics. The Blue struck my neck with an intense energy designed to wrest my attention. The pain lingered in my neck afterward, and the thought of building a relationship with Al Gore pressed on me until I finally decided to act.

In time I came to believe and understand that the Blue, with its sense of urgency and immediacy, was direct communication from God and the Universe—as direct as it gets.

How could I not pay attention?

2
Little Match Girl

Abuse. Spiritual awakening. Loss.

I hesitate to write about these things, but all are crucial to my story, and I can find no way to leave them out. Most people have been through the death of someone they love, have received spiritual insights, or have been abused by those they trust. It is because of such experiences that we grow into the person we are meant to be. Indeed, it is through these experiences that I became *me*.

Why was I so terrified to write a letter to a congressman? How had a lightning bolt found me in the first place? And what enabled me to trust a voice that seemed to come from another world?

Had some divine force led me to this moment, guiding my steps through childhood, difficult and painful as it was, leading me up to the moment of inspiration? Or was all of this random? Had the lightning bolt accidentally touched me on its way out of town?

"Wednesday's child is full of woe." So goes the nursery rhyme. Quite a mantle to place on a child.

I regret to say that in my case the description fit; I was not a happy child. Listening to my mother read tales of Little Red Riding Hood, Cinderella, and Snow White, I believed that they spoke a truth: evil did lurk behind trees, inside mirrors, and in those close to home. As far as I could tell, evil lurked everywhere.

At the age of five, the year I was introduced to fairy tales, I strayed from home one afternoon in search of my father, who had left the house to go to his office. I was sure I could find the office because it stood near the railroad station, and there were tracks not far from our house. I would follow the tracks—how hard could that be? He would be surprised to see me and proud that I was able to figure it out.

I stopped at the house of a four-year-old friend and coaxed her to join me. When we reached the tracks, Janice and I became entranced with the scrap metal inside a box car and played for what must have been a long time. Finally we returned to the tracks, jumping from tie to tie for a couple of blocks, then wandered into a neighborhood in search of a shortcut. Here I chanced upon the school where I was to start kindergarten soon, a place my mother had previously taken me. As the afternoon sky darkened, Janice became frightened and plodded back in the direction we had come. Intent on finding my father, I was lingering, trying to decide which direction to go, when a dog twice my size lunged from a darkened stairwell, baring its teeth and snarling. I was terrified, certain he wanted to eat me. Then, just as suddenly, an older boy appeared and grabbed the dog by the collar, scowling as though I were the menace.

It was 8:00 p.m. when a policeman found me gazing at a theater marquee a half mile from the school and escorted me home in his patrol car. I thought my parents would be happy to see me, but my father led me upstairs to their bedroom, took a hairbrush from the drawer, and spanked me "to teach me a lesson," then sent me to bed without supper. He never asked why I left the house and never knew that I'd gone looking for him. I felt like the brave and innocent Cinderella, maligned and misunderstood.

Years later I wondered why my mother chose to read me fairy tales. All were grim; many had unhappy endings. I followed Little Red Riding Hood through the forest, waiting for the wolf to devour her. I watched as the witch shoved Hansel and Gretel into her oven, and the jealous queen, proclaiming

Snow White too fair, gave her a poisoned apple. If any of these fates were to befall me, I would die. I knew no dwarfs or princes who would come to my rescue.

I feel certain my mother did not understand how these tales affected me. How could she know that I would try to sort out life by these precarious threads? How could she guess that I would identify most closely with the characters who nearly froze to death in winter, the little match girl and the ugly duckling?

The girl wears a tattered coat and no shoes, selling matches for a penny. It is snowing and no one will buy. She crouches against a wall and strikes a match for warmth, then lights another, and another. The third match seems to shine through the wall into a cozy, comfortable home. A bounteous dinner is on the table, the figure of a mother bustling about, and in the corner a candlelit Christmas tree. The girl is filled with excruciating longing.

Elsewhere, a duckling is hatched, but he is unlike the others. They call him ugly and make fun of him. In exasperation, his mother leaves him to wander on his own, only to be rejected by the barnyard animals and the farmer's family. Forced to spend the winter alone, he huddles at the edge of the pond, where he shivers to keep warm and eventually freezes to the ice.

I was the poor, shabby child selling matches and the strange duckling rejected by its mother without help from anyone. I felt that I was dying in a land of ice and snow. How could such stories have a happy ending?

But all was not lost.

The mother sees the match girl through the window and brings her into the house, aglow from the fire in the fireplace. She serves the girl a bowl of soup and tucks her into a feather bed where the girl falls fast asleep. The little match girl is welcomed into the family, where she lives happily ever after.

And when spring comes, the duck spies a flock of beautiful white birds that circle the pond and splash down beside him. The duck bows his head in shame: he is so ugly, and they, so beautiful. Then he glimpses his reflection in the water. He looks just like them! He has become a swan! The others gather around and welcome him as one of their own.

I took these lessons to heart, wanting to believe that no matter how miserable my life was, my story could have a happy ending; that if I persisted, I would find the home I longed for, a family that cherished me, perhaps even kinship with a beautiful swan.

I was not an orphan; I grew up with two parents and a younger sister. But it was an uncertain life, as we traipsed around the country like gypsies, never staying in one place long enough for me to make friends.

My mother was bitterly unhappy. I knew that we moved because of my father's failed business deals and his other women. Both of these were cause enough for her unhappiness. But the repeated moves also unsettled us, forcing us to give up friends and familiar territory over and over. It was not until years later that I uncovered a deeper truth: my father molested me repeatedly, a crime my mother did not see. She was a good mother in many ways, but at his hands and without her help, I was ravaged as a child.

The abuse began when I was two and continued until I was eleven. It was the defining experience of my life, destroying my equilibrium and eating away at my self-esteem. It was couched in baby talk and syrupy affection, which made me feel crazy. My father threatened to kill me if I told, and since I couldn't tell, I was uncertain if it had really happened.

To protect myself, I cut myself off from all memory of the abuse. I became acutely sensitive to the emotions and intentions of others, learning when to be noticed and when to fade into the wall. I was like a radio receiver picking up signals and vibrations from far and wide, then adjusting my behavior as best I could to a complex assortment of cues.

This heightened awareness sharpened my senses of touch and hearing; I cringed at loud noises and drew back when touched. When my father put his hands on me, my consciousness left my body. I stared at the ceiling or out the window, my attention in another reality. I spent so much time out of my body that years later when I learned how to meditate, I could easily alter the focus of my consciousness.

I have heard that Spirit enters a wounded child to mend it and make it whole. Whether this is true, I cannot say. I do know that the process of healing and transformation is a long-term rehabilitation, knitting and purling, back and forth for decades.

My parents fought constantly over my father's girlfriends, extravagant spending, and business failures. The new champagne-colored Cadillac that showed up in our driveway each year infuriated my mother, who often scrimped to keep food on the table. There were women I heard about ("Your mother and I are getting a divorce," my father announced when Cathy was four and I was eight), and there were women I met. One sat in the front seat beside my father the day he drove up with a similar announcement. It was March 18, my father's 36th birthday and—"isn't it amazing?" my father exclaimed—it was this young woman's birthday, too, her 18th.

Despite their unhappiness, neither of my parents attended church. My mother must have thought it important for her daughters, however, because as we crisscrossed the country, she dropped Cathy and me at whichever church was closest to home. Over the years Cathy and I colored and cut out legions of Old Testament figures and played out the stories in Sunday school: David and Goliath, Lot and his wife, Daniel in the lion's den. The stories were as dramatic as fairy tales. I noted that God always rescued his people, but they seemed to be special people, selected for special tasks. Those who obeyed the Lord and relied on him were safe against giants and ferocious animals, and those who did not, God turned into pillars of salt. Sunday school teachers pointed out that the former were God's chosen people, and that I could be one, too, if I accepted Jesus as my savior.

It seemed that Jesus had been sent to save all the people that God hadn't rescued in the Old Testament. His method of saving was confusing to me—dying on a cross so that I could be free—but I liked his miracles and bravery in standing up to the Pharisees. I was comforted when he touched the lepers and treated Mary Magdalene with kindness. I felt Jesus was someone I would like to know, but I felt no personal connection to him.

When I was sixteen, a new minister arrived at the Lutheran church Cathy and I were attending. Pastor Paul had yellow hair that folded back on itself like an envelope and sleepy blue eyes that could see right through you. Tall, broad-shouldered, Norwegian, he strode around our church grounds with serene self-confidence, calling each young person by name. We teens adored him. Unlike other adults in our lives, he talked with us about the real issues we faced and listened to our troubles. In church, with dramatic flair, he confronted the adults who said they believed in Jesus, exhorting them to love and forgive one another, to live what Jesus had said. One year during Lent he dressed up as Jesus' disciples, one per week—Peter, Paul, Mark, and Judas—and admonished us to love even those who had turned against us.

Pastor Paul invited me to be a camp counselor at Big Bear Lake that summer, in the mountains northeast of Los Angeles. I was thrilled to be asked and, even more so, to be part of the special cadre of camp leaders I met the first day of camp. As counselors we were important —in charge of our cottage, and admired by the campers, too.

The counselors, campers, and pastors joked and teased one another from the beginning. The counselors short-sheeted the pastors' cots; the campers short-sheeted ours. We put sugar in the salt shakers, lobbed green Jell-O across the dining room table, and threw each other in the lake. For the first time in my life, I let down my guard.

This gaiety was in stark contrast to my life at home, and the familiarity among campers stirred the embers of my pain. I struggled with my feelings all week—one minute deliriously happy, the next in bottomless grief.

Thursday evening after campfire, darkly depressed about my life, I asked Pastor Paul if I could talk to him. Seeking a private place, we walked downhill to the parking lot and sat in the front seat of his car with the light outside the dining hall shining in our faces.

Once in the car, my tears spilled out.

He watched me, eyes tender, but said nothing, waiting for me to speak.

I gulped back the tears. "My dad's having an affair with his secretary. He went to Las Vegas last week to get a divorce." It was the fourth time I was aware of that he had planned to leave my mother for another woman, although, I learned years later, there were many more.

Pastor Paul took my hand.

"He leaves, then my mother starts throwing up and can't eat anything, and he feels sorry for her and comes back." I was sobbing, unable to hold back the tears. "Sometimes I wish he would stay away for good."

Pastor Paul tilted his head to look into my eyes. "What can I do to help?"

I shook my head. "There's nothing anyone can do."

"Perhaps I could talk to your mother," he said, and I nodded yes because it seemed that talking to my mother might help.

We sat for half an hour, saying little while I wept. Finally we walked up the hill to our cabins and said goodnight. I crept into bed, my heart aching with pain. Outside the screened windows, the stars peeked through the pines, comforting me. I watched the stars and listened to the crickets until the sky became light.

In the morning I felt scraped raw inside and could barely

talk to anyone. I muddled through the day. That evening the camp gathered in the dining hall to watch a film. On a huge screen over our heads loomed the figure of Jesus in a white robe, face glowing, his pale eyes penetrating mine. "Jesus loves us all," a voice said. "He loved us so much that he gave his life for us."

Jesus spoke, palms open, arms outstretched. "Love one another as I have loved you." I was mesmerized and felt as though my heart would burst. Pastor Paul and Jesus seemed to merge and become one.

With the image of Jesus still on the screen, Pastor Paul talked about love and serving others, then read from the Gospel of Matthew: "Truly I say unto you, as you did it to one of the least of these my brethren, you did it to me." He asked us to make a commitment to serve others because that was what Jesus wanted of us and it was what Jesus had done. The pastors passed around a book for us to sign our names, to go on record as those who would serve God.

In my cabin that night, flashlight in hand, I wrote in the margin next to Matthew 25:40, "This will be my golden rule."

Concerned about my home life, Pastor Paul urged my mother to send me to a Christian college away from home. To her credit and my good fortune, she listened. There were no Lutheran colleges in California, but my parents agreed to send me to St. Olaf College in Northfield, Minnesota, where a high school friend would be going. It was a stunningly beautiful campus with gray stone buildings that towered over lush rolling lawns. The college was proud of its choir, the magnificent organ that resounded in the chapel, and its high academic standards.

I loved the music and traditions of St. Olaf, but I struggled academically. I made the mistake of signing up for Russian and advanced calculus my freshman year, confident I could handle them because I had excelled in high school, but the course load was overwhelming. Still, my golden rule stirred inside me. When a group of seniors announced they would visit the homes of mentally ill people to sing Christmas carols, I volunteered to join them.

On a gray, dreary day, the fields blanketed with snow, ten of us rode in a van to visit three sites. We caroled in front of two buildings as large as manor homes, where a few staff stood at the door, but we never saw those who lived there. Late in the afternoon, as the sun sank behind clouds, we arrived at a small brick building close to the road. There were just two small windows high up. We stood in the yard and sang to those windows, with no response from within. A deep sadness overcame me. Who was inside, I wondered, and what must their lives be like? I had seen Olivia DeHavilland in *The Snake Pit* and imagined terrible things going on in that building, people screaming in pain and confusion and lying in their own excrement. I believe to this day that my fears were probably close to the truth.

The following year California Lutheran College opened its doors just sixty miles from home. From my parents' point of view, there was no question that I would transfer, as St. Olaf was too expensive and too far away.

I didn't want to leave St. Olaf and the friends I had made, but attending CLC was one of the best things that could have happened to me. I studied literature, art, and world religions, learned more about serving others, and developed a deep sense of devotion. With less than two hundred students the first year, the college became my longed-for family as well as a laboratory where I could learn how to be a leader. I served on the student council, represented the college at meetings on distant campuses, and, as a junior, organized a visitation program to the nearby mental hospital.

One-fourth of CLC's then-400 students signed up to visit wards at Camarillo State Hospital once a month. The buildings were prisons, dark, colorless, with huge metal gates and locks and chains on every door. The lounges where we visited the residents were little better. We brought cookies, sang songs, and talked with the residents one-on-one. We never knew what impact we had, but it felt very important that we went.

Out of college, I mustered my courage and joined the Peace Corps, eager to respond to President Kennedy's call to serve our country. I wanted to be of service, but also to distance myself from my father's values that placed money and things above people. His materialism echoed what I saw in the culture around me, and I felt a desperate need to view life from a different perspective.

My two-year assignment was teaching English in a boys' secondary school in Thailand. When not at school, I immersed myself in the Buddhist culture, visiting temples, conversing with monks, and attending Buddhist weddings and funerals. *Mai pen rai,* said the Thais about every irritation or difficulty that came along. *Let it go, it doesn't matter.* This spiritual teaching both puzzled and inspired me. I came to love the students I worked with and became convinced that, contrary to what I'd been taught in church, all the Thais were not going to hell. Jesus had said he was the truth, the light, and the way, but I had to believe that there were other truths, other lights, other ways.

By the time I left Thailand, I had begun studying the writings of men who integrated the religious thought of East and West: Alan Watts, Joseph Campbell, and later Ram Dass. I learned yoga and meditation, becoming aware of feelings of peace and happiness that I could touch within me and the energy that flowed through my body. Over and over I experienced God as the energy that existed within me as well as without.

For much of my life it was my sister Cathy I loved the most. We had weathered the storms on the home front together, sailing our little boat over those tempestuous seas. We were sailors huddled against the winds of our father's affairs and buffeted by our family's constant moves.

As it turned out, she was also the one who opened me most

to Spirit. Four years younger than I, she was the confirmation that I existed. When I doubted my reality, I could look into those luscious dark eyes with eyelashes like Da Vinci's arcs of ink, those sweeps of dark, dark brown—opening and closing, looking back at me. I knew then that no matter what happened, life could go on. In her, I saw a reflection of my own tender life—a freer, more impetuous version of me.

In order to tolerate the tension at home, Cathy and I created other lives, other families: paper doll sisters who lived in paper doll houses, grass nests in the vacant lot next door, shelters made of blankets hung between trees in canyons. These were sanctuaries for Hansel and Gretel, away from the wicked witch of the forest, where we made our own rules and nurtured ourselves with story books, apples, and cookies.

We worked jigsaw puzzles of autumn leaves held brightly on trees and became storyland characters that traded gumdrops for ice cream cones. We made card trails that looped across the carpet and up the stairs, leading the other into a potted plant or a musty closet. We gave names and voices to small ceramic animals that lived in houses we designed on felt-covered boards.

Transported to imaginary lands, we'd forget Mother and Daddy in the next room. We were Molly the squirrel and Debbie the deer, buying groceries, sweeping the porch, and fixing fried chicken and apple pie.

While I went away to college and joined the Peace Corps, Cathy finished high school, got married, and became pregnant. When I returned to the States in 1967, I found that Cathy and her husband had moved to Oakland, California, to be near her husband's family. She worked the night shift at a bank for the next several years and raised her son.

Cathy was thirty-two when a bone tumor was discovered in her right hip. She had just finished her master's degree and started working as a school psychologist. Within weeks she had to quit her job. In January 1979 she was diagnosed with fourth-stage histiocytic lymphoma, her hips and spine riddled with tumors. Her prognosis was very poor.

I had married three years earlier and moved to Tennessee to attend graduate school. After Cathy's diagnosis, I visited her in California every other weekend, and she and I talked daily on the phone. I agonized as she underwent a horrendous regimen of radiation and chemotherapy. After each treatment, we would all pray, hoping her white blood count would rise again so that they could conduct the next round. She saw a psychologist who taught her to visualize white blood cells killing the cancer cells, tiny white knights vanquishing the foe. She was valiantly cheerful for three months, then she became discouraged and gave up.

Throughout this time I openly grieved for the one person I had thought would go on with me, the one I thought would never die. I flew to see Cathy for two weeks in June and two weeks again in July as she drifted toward death. She was emaciated, her belly swollen; each day brought more and more pain. Her dark brown curls had disappeared, replaced by a cotton scarf. She spent most of the day in a twin bed that had been pushed up against the living room windows.

One afternoon as I sat at Cathy's bedside, thinking her asleep, her voice startled me. "Wait," she said.

I looked up from the book I was reading. "What is it, Cat?"

She raised her head off the pillow and held herself still, listening to something I could not hear.

"There's a voice. Out there." She lifted her arm and pointed out the window in the direction of a small cemetery about a mile away. "Someone's calling me." Her voice quivered. "Someone's saying, 'Come with me. It's okay, you're coming home.'"

I watched, astonished, as her head dropped back onto the pillow, eyes closed, tears gathering under her lashes. She mouthed the words, "It's okay. Come with me."

When she opened her eyes, a single tear began to slide down each cheek. Glancing at me, she smiled the wry smile she saved for moments of paradox or great meaning. "Your sister's going home," she said.

Our family had moved to San Clemente, California, when I was twelve and Cathy was eight. She and I spent the next five summers at the beach, basking in the sun, diving headfirst into the waves, exploring sand crabs, shells, and kelp, and bracing ourselves against the surf. It was our training ground for growing physically strong and ready to tackle life. Both of us thrilled to the power of the waves, the constant movement of tides, and the ocean depths. Assuming the role in our lives once filled by paper doll houses, vacant lots, and canyons, the beach offered images and sensory experiences that remained with us long into adulthood.

Seven days before she died, Cathy dreamed she was on a beach gazing out to sea, where the sun shone deep into the water. She sat under a palm tree, lulled by the lapse between waves, her eyes shaded by a wide-brimmed straw hat. She felt happy and content, as though she belonged there. At the end of the dream she glanced up the beach to a row of brown-shingled houses that faced the water.

During her waking hours Cathy was usually in pain and frightened about what was happening to her. When she awoke that day she felt happy for the first time in months. The sensation lingered for most of the morning. Later she told me she wanted to sleep, because there she could be at peace.

Two nights later she dreamed that a real estate agent was showing her the houses. Cathy and the realtor went inside each one, walked through the rooms, and climbed the stairs to the second floor. Each house had picture windows where the sun spilled onto the wood floors. Through the windows, Cathy looked out to the beach and the taffeta sea that rippled beyond. Quiet and peaceful, the houses nurtured a longing she'd felt all her life. Once she had seen them all, she chose the place where she wanted to live and signed a contract.

We laughed about this dream, how perfect in its detail:

the gleaming wood floors, the rippling sea, and a real estate contract.

Then there was another: She stood in front of the house she had chosen, her back to the sea. In her palm she clasped a key. She walked up the front steps, turned the key, and swung open the door, letting in a splash of sunlight. In the corner she found a broom and began sweeping out the house, making it ready to move in.

A fourth and final dream came the morning before she died. She and the realtor had made another appointment. When the realtor arrived, the two of them looked at the houses again, this time to find places for Mother, my husband Ron, and me to live when we joined her.

Cathy had asked the doctors what her death would be like. When they told her she would likely have a bowel obstruction or a brain tumor, both difficult and very painful, Cathy decided that when the end was near, she would take sleeping pills while she could still keep them down. A doctor friend gave her a prescription.

Mother, Ron, and I were all staying with Cathy and her husband Matt when she called us individually to her bedside to ask what we would think of someone who took her own life. We each told her, not knowing what the others said, that we would support her decision. If she decided to take the pills, we wanted to be with her. After speaking to each of us, Cathy announced she would take the pills the following weekend, while we were all at the house.

On Sunday Cathy woke early, and I along with her. Sparrows twittered in the acacia trees outside her window as the sky turned to light. Matt and I were taking turns sleeping in the living room near her bed. That night we both slept nearby: Matt in a sleeping bag on the floor and I on the couch.

Matt heard us whispering and climbed out of the sleeping bag to join me at her bedside. "I'm ready to do it," Cathy said. There was little emotion in her voice.

I took her hand. "Are you sure, Cat?" Matt asked her, too.

"Yes." She nodded. "I'm sure."

Cathy and I watched Matt slowly stack pieces of wood in the fireplace and light a fire. Ron and Mother joined us and stood silently by. Then Matt went to the kitchen and returned with a tray that held a pitcher full of water and five glasses. He poured water into the glasses and handed one to each of us.

Cathy pushed back the blankets and gingerly eased herself onto the floor. She propped herself against the bed and shifted so that her weight was on her left hip. "Ah, that's better," she said. Her waif-like frame, so fragile now, looked almost transparent in the morning light.

Matt handed Cathy the vial of pills, and she began to count them out: twenty-five, thirty, thirty-five. Such tiny, innocent-looking pills. Then she began taking them, a handful at a time, before any of us could say anything. We watched and sipped from our glasses in silence.

At one point Ron choked on the water and coughed.

Cathy looked up. "A little fear, perhaps?" she said. We all laughed nervously.

Cathy finished taking the pills and placed the vial on the floor. Then she raised her fist into the air and exclaimed, a victorious smile on her face, "I did it!" She crawled into the sleeping bag and said, simply, "Good night."

The four of us gathered around Cathy. We touched her, told her we loved her, cried, and told stories about her life. All the while, she slept, her face sweet and peaceful.

The doctor had said that the pills would take four or five hours to stop her heart. At five hours she was still alive, although her breathing had changed several times. We became frightened that the pills might not work and that she would wake up brain-damaged. We were exhausted, and everyone decided to lie down. Mother and Matt went upstairs while Ron and I stayed with Cathy.

At six hours, Ron and I noticed another shift in her breathing. I got up and went to the kitchen for more water.

As the water filled my glass, I was startled by the sound of laughter pealing through the house, and the loud flapping of wings. It was joyous, bright. I turned quickly in the direction of the sound and my glass crashed to the floor.

Then I knew. It was the sound of Cathy's soul leaving her body. My sister was free at last.

Cathy had cancer in her bones, and three months before she died I developed a sympathetic bone tumor. Mine was benign, but it consumed three-quarters of the thickness of my tibia. It required surgery, which I arranged for after her death. I would be on crutches for six months.

The bone tumor was a poignant reminder of how close we had been, but it paled next to how I felt in my heart: I wanted to die to be with her. The full force of it hit me the day after the funeral, stunning me with raw, unbridled violence.

I awoke early and drove to the cemetery. It would be my last chance to be with Cathy before Ron and I returned to Tennessee. I needed to talk to her, to find out if she was all right.

Kneeling beside the grave, I saw through the soil to her body below, to the face that was so at peace when she died, her fingers interlaced across her chest, the flowered dress, and the Chinese dragon slippers, my earlier gift to her that we had placed on her delicate, pointed feet. I knelt for a long while, then walked in ever-widening circles among the grave sites nearby, reading names and dates on each marker. I wanted to know if there were others who had died young, too, others to keep her company. I found a few—a nineteen-year-old who had died in action in Vietnam, a three-year-old girl, and a baby.

When I returned to her grave, I immediately became agitated. Grief mounted inside me, rising like a squall.

"Take care of my sister, damn it!" I shook my fist at

the cloudless sky, which beamed down at me blank and unresponsive.

"Take care of my sister," I sobbed.

Sitting on a low stone wall, I wept, my heart crushed, for what seemed like a very long time.

After a while, I stopped to catch my breath. "Cathy, are you here? Are you all right?"

"Give me a sign," I implored the trees overhead. Quiescent, the cemetery seemed to be listening to me. "Please give me a sign!"

In that instant, I heard a noise to my right and turned, startled, to see a small yellow cat jump out from behind a tombstone to fix me in its gaze.

I gasped out loud. "Cat!"

We looked at each other, amazed. *Where did you come from?* I puzzled, staring at its poised frame. I had walked through the entire area and had not seen a cat. For several seconds it stared at me, unblinking. Then it began to run. It scampered across graves, around tombstones, and up the hill until it was out of sight.

It was the first of many visits from Cathy's spirit to help me heal. I would speak her name when I lay down at night, and she would appear as a presence I could sense across the room. Then she drew nearer until she nestled against my chest. I believe that she talked to me and held me, often staying until I fell asleep. These visits were like warm oil bathing my bruised soul. She visited me for almost a year and only left when I could finally let her go.

The visits by Cathy's spirit, like the voice outside her window, her dreams of the ocean, the pealing of laughter, and the appearance of a yellow cat, were strange at first, but in time I came to accept them as natural. I had joined Cathy in the spiritual initiation of her death. I shared in that initiation, walking to the portal with her, holding her hand as she stepped across. I was so close to her in her dying that I had experienced the portal opening up.

Job Description.

Cathy's death opened a door to the world of Spirit for me. During the months that I grieved, the door remained open, allowing Cathy's spirit to visit me often. I had no idea that this door would lead me into the political realm. It was many years before I understood the connection between the experiences surrounding Cathy's death and the bolt from the blue.

It would have helped to have an inkling of what was to come, perhaps a job description tacked to the door: *Person needed for role in political arena, to be played out in the halls of Congress, directed from the world of Spirit.*

In the four years after Cathy's death, and before lightning struck in Louise's living room, perhaps I could have trained for the job.

The lightning bolt left me terrified and disbelieving. Surely I had not been singled out. Surely God had not spoken to me through this electric charge. Yet I sensed that something real had happened and that the impact on my life would be great. The only other lightning bolt experience I knew about was Saul on the road to Damascus, an event that transformed Saul into Saint Paul and converted him from a persecutor of Christians to an Apostle of the Christian Church. The event turned his life upside down.

I did not dare believe that *my* life would be turned upside down, too.

3
Wings

After writing the first letter to Al Gore, I shook with terror for weeks, not fully understanding why. I sensed that I had been shown—by the Universe, by God, by my own psyche perhaps—a doorway through which I could step. Yet I knew that if I crossed that threshold, I would face the waves of fear my actions stirred up.

I was afraid to fly, afraid that if I flew too high, my wings would melt, like those of Icarus, and I would be dashed to Earth. Take a role in the political arena? Become friends with a member of Congress? Not me! I was terrified of what would be required of me. I wanted to make a difference in the world, but I didn't want that much responsibility. Despite my Ph.D. in educational policy and a brief stint as chair of a legislative committee in California, I felt ill-prepared for the task.

I was certain that no one in the arms control arena would take me seriously. I had two strikes against me: I was female, and I was not an expert in law, science, arms control, or politics. In Washington, expertise in problem-solving, promoting human values, grassroots organizing, and personal empowerment—areas where I excelled—was generally discounted. Because I had never worked in the arena of arms control, I felt certain my thinking would be dismissed.

My friends and my Nashville disarmament group cheered me on. Their encouragement was crucial to my going forward, but by itself it was not enough. It was Re-evaluation Counseling

(RC), a peer counseling network Ron and I had joined years earlier, that enabled me to enter the political realm.

The basic concept of RC is that releasing one's feelings through crying, shaking, angry movement, and talking leads to clearer, more effective, thinking. Once painful emotions from a past incident are released, one can re-evaluate the incident, which is where RC gets its name. It is this healing process that children follow naturally unless a well-meaning adult steps in and urges them to stop.

RC is also known as co-counseling because one person is client and the other counselor, then they reverse roles. At the end of a counseling session, each participant decides on a specific action to take during the following week, based on material he or she has discussed in the session. Taking action brings up more feelings, which can be worked on in the next counseling session, thus propelling an ongoing cycle of personal growth.

It was a powerful tool, one that had consistently worked for me and for hundreds of others I knew. It was more powerful and left me feeling more in control of my life than psychotherapy, which I had tried in the previous decade. Ron was involved in RC when I met him, and shortly afterwards he became certified to teach. Within a year I was certified as well, and both of us went on to teach for over a dozen years. Two years after I started co-counseling, I had felt a significant shift in my ability to think clearly. In time I worked through lifelong feelings of isolation, and when Cathy was dying, I became less and less fearful of death.

Prior to my becoming involved in the Nuclear Freeze movement, I had attended a workshop where RC's international leader, Harvey Jackins, called on all co-counselors to set aside time in their counseling sessions to talk about and release feelings related to nuclear weapons and the threat of nuclear war. Harvey knew that by doing so, people would work through their numbness on this issue and be ready to take action in some way. Indeed, after just two twenty-minute sessions, I made the decision that I would do what I could to eliminate nuclear weapons in the world.

When I began to work with Al Gore, I counseled on the letters I was writing and the phone calls I was making, in each session trembling with fear. At the end of each session, my painful feelings had lessened and I felt ready to take the next step.

In early July, two weeks after my first letter to Gore, I attended a Re-evaluation Counseling workshop in Chicago led by Harvey himself. An important aspect of RC workshops is the leader counseling participants in front of the group, which serves to demonstrate effective counseling as well as to assist individuals in working through their painful feelings. Although I had attended numerous workshops in the previous eight years, the Chicago workshop was the first where participants talked about being sexually abused as children. My own memories of abuse had long ago settled into obscurity, but hearing others speak of their experiences brought my memories to the surface, as though dredging them up from the ocean floor, the debris of an ancient wreck.

As others talked, an unknown terror began to build inside me until I felt I was going to scream. It was time for the workshop to end for the evening, but I waved my hand frantically and begged Harvey to work with me. In the half hour that ensued, he asked repeatedly what had happened to me. A string of seven memories bubbled up, one after the other. As I talked, I was horrified that the words flowed from my mouth and stunned into disbelief.

According to RC theory, old hurts profoundly limit our responses in the present. I understood that my memories had languished, waiting for a time when I was ready to face what had happened and to start working through them. In taking the first step with Gore and beginning to release old feelings of powerlessness, what surfaced were memories of abuse. My psyche was offering them up: "Here is what robbed you of power. Here is where you can do the work to empower yourself."

Many things began to make sense: why as an adolescent and young adult I was terrified of men; why on several occasions certain men sensed my vulnerability and tried to rape or kill me; why I cringed when my father touched me; why I hated him so much. My feelings of powerlessness in the political world came from my father abusing me and telling me that he would kill me if I spoke the truth. How dare I "speak truth to power," a popular tenet of social change, when my survival seemed at stake?

After returning from Chicago, my "dream self" offered an indication that the process of empowerment had already begun. In the dream, I was attending a conference on a college campus, where Gore had come to speak.

I'm sitting near the front, but I think Al Gore can't see me, and I want to ask him for my "hour" with him. He shifts in his seat, smiles, and begins joking with me.

The meeting ends and I leave to go back to my car, which is in a parking lot far away. It is night and semi-dark as I walk up the hill. When I reach the parking lot, Gore is playing in the snow with a group of women, who are throwing snowballs at each other. He invites me to join in the play.

Ron and Phillip, one of my co-counseling partners, appear. I hook elbows with Ron on my right, Phillip on my left, with Gore directly in front of me. We become a "team" against the women's team.

Then we decide to fly. We walk into the wind, moving as though we are a single organism. We speed up, run faster and faster, our arms and fingers outstretched. Our fingers are the feathers of our wings. I wake up as we are about to take off.

The feeling in the dream was one of liberation and great power. By joining with Ron, whom I experienced as supportive, in touch with nature, down-to-earth; Phillip, who was emotionally open and sensitive; and Gore, who was becoming more and more powerful in the world, I would be able to fly. In my waking life, Gore was like a fire igniting my personal and political power. The dream suggested that a new, integrated self was preparing to "take off." The ultimate power and freedom would come when I left the ground and took to the air.

That fall of 1983, the magical quality of the dream infused

my days. I kept my commitment of writing a letter once a month, presenting our group's positions on various arms control measures and asking questions to try to understand Gore's thinking. Why did he vote a certain way? What was his intention in supporting the ten-warhead MX missile? Gradually my questions went deeper to what motivated him, and what were his dreams and his vision for the world.

During this time I talked to Peter Knight often, as well as to Aaron Wolfe, a defense analyst who advised Gore on arms control policy. I learned that Gore's staff often forwarded my letters to Wolfe for his review.

Eighteen months before Gore's MX vote, he had asked Wolfe to put together a series of briefings on nuclear weapons. During those eighteen months, Gore and five other congressmen participated in weekly briefings that Wolfe organized for the purpose of developing a new approach to arms control policy. Their goal was to devise an alternative that would break the pattern of the escalating U.S.-U.S.S.R. nuclear arms race.

Aaron Wolfe and I had spoken on the phone a couple of times before I met him as well as Peter on my trip to Washington that October. It was my maiden voyage to Washington, launched and paid for by the Nashville Freeze group.

At Gore's office in the Longworth House Office Building, I introduced myself to the receptionist.

"Oh, yes!" She beamed. "We've talked on the phone many times. I'll let Peter know you're here."

Moments later Peter entered the waiting area and extended his hand, smiling brightly. He was of medium build, perhaps thirty-five, with black hair and lively blue eyes. "Great to finally meet you, Caroline. Come on back."

We sat at his desk while he telephoned Aaron to let him know I was there, then turned to me. "Al's looking forward to talking with you. He wants to get your response to one of his proposals."

"That's great." I nodded. "People in the Freeze group are pleased with Al's letter about anti-satellite weapons." By now I called him Al when talking with Peter, who always used the congressman's first name.

A sandy-haired man in his late forties strode into the office fast, head down. Peter introduced us, and Aaron nodded from behind thick glasses, polite but abrupt.

We took the stairs to the basement cafeteria, Peter friendly and cheerful—ebullient, in fact. He told me how much they appreciated my efforts to communicate Gore's positions to the folks back home. Aaron appeared to listen intently, averting his eyes and saying nothing.

Once we'd gone through the cafeteria line and found a table, Aaron briefly presented Gore's arms control positions. His manner was cool and brusque. Our discussion centered on a "build down" proposal that some members of Congress, including Gore, were offering as an alternative to a Freeze. The idea was that the U.S. should build the Midgetman, the single-warhead missile that Gore had mentioned in our first meeting, before trying to negotiate with the Soviets for reductions. It made no sense to me, given that the U.S. and Soviet Union had over 50,000 nuclear weapons between them and the U.S. was ahead of the Soviet Union in speed of weapons as well as technology.

Wolfe and Gore saw the Midgetman as a way to "stabilize" the arms race; eventually each missile could only hit one target. "Once we build the Midgetman, we can get rid of the bigger ones with multiple warheads," Gore had said. The National Freeze movement opposed this proposal on several grounds. Building more weapons would cost billions of dollars, increase the overall numbers of weapons, and give no assurance that reductions would follow. But, intimidated by Wolfe's manner, I listened and protested only mildly.

Wolfe claimed the Freeze movement was stirring people up—he singled out Helen Caldicott, a fiery Australian physician who had become a spokesperson for nuclear disarmament—which was why people feared that nuclear holocaust was just around the corner. He was angry that I had fallen in line with the popular sentiment, angry that he had to deal with me at all.

I asked about Gore's underlying assumptions, why he had developed an approach that called for building more weapons as a way of reducing the threat. Wolfe's answer was complex and full of technological terms, which I followed as best I could. As he talked, it became clear to me that he and Gore were very close, that there was a deep respect and caring between them. I thought that if Gore were ever elected president, this man would be his national security advisor.

I felt Wolfe examining me closely. *He may be defensive and crusty,* I thought, *but I feel certain I can break through that crust.* I determined to do what I could to earn his confidence.

After two hours we returned to Gore's office, where Peter suggested that I wait in the reception area. He emerged shortly to say that Gore was on the House floor for a series of votes; Gore had called and asked if they would send me over to the Rayburn Room. Peter assigned an intern to accompany me through the labyrinth of corridors and subways to the Capitol building.

I spotted Gore in the hallway just off the House floor. He stopped for several seconds and stared, as though uncertain if this was the person he was meeting. I learned later that he wore glasses, but not in public, so perhaps he couldn't make out if it was me. Then he strode quickly, making his way through the clumps of congressmen and lobbyists to where I stood. "How *are* you?" he asked warmly.

We entered the high-ceilinged Rayburn Room, an elegantly furnished anteroom just a few yards from the voting chambers of the House of Representatives. I followed Gore to armchairs in a corner away from the noise, where he asked me to wait. When he returned, his beeper went off, and he listened intently to announcements of upcoming votes.

"How much time do we have?" I asked.

He studied his watch. "About fifteen minutes till they call for the next vote."

"Shall I begin?"

He nodded. "Please."

"We would like an opportunity to work with you on a number of arms control measures. Specifically, we're very concerned about the deployments of Pershing missiles in Europe."

As I described the Freeze strategy, he listened intently, nodding at key points. Then he suggested several possible projects we could work on together ("for example, my amendment to cut funds for anti-satellite weapons") and told me of a proposal he was considering for the deployments in Europe.

"I know that isn't exactly what you were looking for." He watched my face for a reaction. "But do you like this proposal?"

I needed time to think about it and to discuss it with my colleagues back home, and told him so.

"I really value your friendship," he said.

The beeper went off a second time. He excused himself and again asked me to wait. I glanced at my watch. We'd been talking for half an hour.

When he returned, he asked if I would accompany him to the committee room where he was expected next.

We made the trek through the underground passages, taking escalators and a tram to another of the House office buildings. Along the way, he introduced me to several congressmen. "This is Caroline Cottom," he said proudly, as though they should know who I was.

In the hallway outside the committee room, he said there would be "a gaggle of people" questioning him there and asked what my plans were for the rest of the afternoon.

"I'm scheduled to meet with Rep. Boner's aide in fifteen minutes, but I've left my overnight bag in your office, and I'm completely lost!"

Gore proceeded to give me directions that involved several turns, escalators, and two or three flights of stairs. When I shook my head in confusion and laughed, he pulled a tiny notebook from his pocket and drew a minute, detailed map, small enough to fit on the back of a postage stamp. I laughed again.

We hugged goodbye. "Thanks for everything," he said.

"Yes," I said, "and you, too."

Doug Landers, Rep. Boner's defense aide, met me in the reception area to Boner's office. He was stocky with a beige look: bland plastic-framed glasses, light brown hair, tan shirt and pants. He introduced himself curtly and asked me to follow him.

I had spoken with Landers earlier in the fall and knew that he, like Wolfe, was angry with the Freeze movement. Prior to the Freeze vote in May—the vote that preceded Gore's MX vote—national disarmament organizations lobbied hard to get Rep. Boner on board. Landers was irate. "These Washington lobbyists equated the Freeze with motherhood and apple pie," he had told me on the phone. "We had no choice but to vote for it." It was clear that Boner was not inclined to support arms control measures and didn't like being pressured to do so.

Landers led me into Boner's office, a large room, perhaps 20' x 25', which was empty except for a mahogany desk, a mock oriental carpet, and forty straight-back chairs lining the perimeter. Landers directed me to sit near the door, then selected a seat for himself against the far wall, twenty-five feet away. He leaned back on the rear legs of his chair, crossed his arms, and glowered at me. "So what can I do for you?"

I told him that our group hoped to find some points of common interest with Boner, arms control issues where we could agree. I said I was aware that he and Boner had had a bad experience at the time of the Freeze vote, and I was sorry about that—at which point Landers began to rail at me. How unfairly they'd been treated, how Bill Boner tried to listen to his constituents, but these Washington groups thought *they* elected the congressman. Well, they didn't, and they had no right to pressure Boner to vote against his better judgment.

The carpet was a paisley sea between us, and Landers floating, ranting, so far away. He looked small and obscure.

When he stopped to catch his breath, I leaned forward. "I'm sorry to hear that. What else did they say?" This brought another tirade.

After twenty minutes, Landers suddenly stopped. He eased the front legs of his chair back onto the floor and dropped his arms. Then, as though confused, he glanced around the room. "I'm sorry. I didn't mean to dump all that on you."

Landers proceeded to tell me about Bill Boner, what Boner cared about, and what we as a constituent group could do to get his attention. Namely, Landers said, we could demonstrate that we had the support of Nashville business leaders and professional people for our issues. "He listens to his constituents," he said more than once.

When we finished, Landers escorted me to the front room, shook my hand warmly, and invited me to come again sometime.

Louise and I planned to attend the annual conference of the Nuclear Weapons Freeze Campaign in St. Louis in early December. Upon our return, the Nashville Freeze would send me to Washington to seek reactions from Gore and Senator Jim Sasser to the new national Freeze strategy and to discuss the U.S.-Soviet START talks, which were stalled over the U.S. plan to deploy Pershing missiles in Europe. Meanwhile, our group would pull together a delegation of community leaders to request a meeting with Rep. Boner in his Nashville office.

The day before Louise and I left, I called Peter Knight and learned he was out of the office because his wife had just had a baby. Aaron Wolfe was also unavailable, and the receptionist said she would let him know that I called. I had written a note to Aaron appreciating his candor and willingness to talk with me so openly, an earnest attempt on my part to invite a cordial relationship. I was interested in seeing how he had received this olive branch.

The following day, as we were about to leave for St. Louis, the telephone rang. "This is Aaron," he said soberly. I was surprised that he had called me, surprised to hear his voice.

I was nervous, but focused on the task, asking questions about Rep. AuCoin's build-down figures, which Aaron answered, and expressing concerns about Gore's Euro missiles (Pershing missiles) proposal.

Aaron was astonished that Gore had told me about the proposal. "Word cannot get out about this."

"I've discussed it only with our executive committee. Al knew I would talk to them. I'll ask them to take it no further."

This seemed to mollify him, as he mentioned my recent letter and thanked me for "its—well," he paused, "its tone."

"You're welcome. I meant what I said."

"So I gather."

"There's one more thing. I'm concerned about the article by Garthoff, the sovietologist. You've seen it?"

"Yes, of course," Aaron said.

"About his discussion of the mutual distrust between the U.S. and the Soviet Union?" Aaron's hawkish stance placed fear of the Soviets far ahead of fear of nuclear holocaust. From his point of view, negotiation was practically impossible. "Aaron, I know that mutual fear is a primary concern of Gore's, too. But it seems that we're at the place where somebody's got to take a first step, and it may not be the Soviets."

"I hear what you're saying." His voice seemed very somber. "Point taken."

Aaron told me that our call had made him late for a lunch appointment, but he stayed on the phone a while longer. Then he invited me to call him whenever I'd like.

I sailed to St. Louis, happy that Aaron had responded positively to my note and was open to talking to me.

At the Freeze Conference, activists from around the country voted on a new national strategy, agreeing unanimously on five legislative priorities for 1984. In dozens of workshops, they also shared organizing ideas they were using in their work.

Louise, who had learned to co-counsel in one of my RC classes, was eager to begin organizing house meetings and door-to-door canvassing using the listening tools of RC. We discovered that hundreds, perhaps thousands, of co-counselors had become involved in the Nuclear Freeze, and many had also become leaders. Directors of several statewide Freeze campaigns were using their counseling sessions to clear their thinking and improve their leadership skills. As a consequence of Harvey Jackins' challenge to co-counselors to counsel on ending the nuclear arms race, many had stepped into leadership roles.

Louise and I talked excitedly on the ride home, eager to share our new ideas with people in Nashville. I looked forward to working with Paul to plan our group's involvement in the 1984 legislative and electoral strategy.

On December 6, the day after we returned, I called Gore's office to see if I could get an appointment before the holidays. I knew there were only a couple of weeks left and that getting an appointment would be a long shot, but worth the try.

Peter's voice came on the line. "Hey, Caroline!"

"Peter! Congratulations on your new baby. How is everyone?"

"Oh, thanks! Doing well. Gail's fine, and Zachary's healthy, too. All we could ask for."

"I hope you'll have pictures the next time I'm up for a visit."

He laughed. "You bet I will!"

"Did Aaron tell you we talked last week? I thought we had an excellent conversation."

"Yes, he did. He was pleased with it, too."

"Peter, our Freeze group is sending me to Washington to discuss 1984 legislative strategy as well as our involvement in Gore's Senate race. Is it possible to get an appointment with Gore before Christmas?" These words were much more confident than I felt. It seemed too much for me to ask for another time with Gore so soon.

Peter put me on hold while he talked to Gore's scheduler. "Hey," he said when he came back on the line, "he'll only be in town one day between now and Christmas. But of course we'll make time in his schedule. For you, we have time. For you, we'll work it out."

Peter paused. "You know, you're a remarkable woman—a remarkable person, really. Committed and compassionate. And caring. You're the kind of person we'd like to have working beside us, in whatever way possible."

When I shared Peter's comments with Louise, she said it was all very new, both for me and for them; that no one had ever related to them like this, and therefore it was very hopeful.

On December 15, Peter escorted me into Gore's office to wait while Gore reviewed a press release with a staff member in the outer office. I looked at the pictures on his walls: mostly photos and paintings by Tennessee artists. In a prominent spot above Gore's desk was a large sepia print of Daniel in the lions' den. Below, on a table, a Bible lay open, a red bookmark holding the place. I knew Gore's Southern Baptist faith was very important to him—his beliefs, his prayer life, his personal relationship with God.

I was studying the sepia print when Gore arrived.

"That's how I feel sometimes." It was dark in the office, and his face seemed dark, too.

"Being in politics?"

He nodded. "I keep this picture to remind me that when things got really tough, God took care of Daniel."

"I hope it never gets that bad."

He frowned, as though it was already that bad, and motioned for me to sit down. "What brings you to Washington?" The words were cordial enough, but his tone implied, "Again, so soon?"

So it *was* presumptuous to ask for time with him just two months after the last meeting. Perhaps I should have settled for a phone conversation with Aaron.

I explained my agenda: The Freeze Campaign's 1984 legislative strategy and our local group's role in his Senate campaign. Specifically, I wanted to know how the Freeze strategy meshed with his.

He answered my questions openly, but he was preoccupied, his eyes glassy. *Of course, the demands on his time are legion. He's overwhelmed with things I have no way of knowing about.* The last thing I wanted was to be an added burden. We ended the discussion after fifteen minutes.

When I saw Peter afterward, I asked about Al's glazed look. "Oh, yeah." He nodded grimly. "That's a part of Al Gore not everyone gets to see. But sure, he gets like that."

I had returned to Washington partly to confirm that Aaron had changed in his attitude toward me. Indeed, he had set aside an hour and a half to meet with me, asking questions about the Freeze position and elaborating further about Gore's proposals.

I asked Aaron why he was interested in meeting with me. He gave five reasons, three of which had to do with the tone of the note I wrote him. He was impressed that Gore trusted me so much, that I seemed to be open-minded, and that I had responded to his "nastiness" with kindness. Throughout our meeting, he shared information with a tone of confidentiality and openness and took my hand for a moment before I left.

For the rest of the day I was buoyed by the change in Aaron's demeanor and the currents of Capitol Hill. Peter and I discussed roles the Nashville Freeze group might play in Al's Senate campaign, with Peter offering me several ideas to take home. I ate lunch in the Longworth Building cafeteria, then hiked to the other side of the Hill to meet with John Green, Senator Sasser's defense aide.

Jim Sasser was a supporter of the Nuclear Weapons Freeze who consistently voted for arms control legislation, so the meeting with John Green was relaxed and friendly. We discussed the new strategy, as well as ways people back home could support Sasser in his votes. Specifically, the senator requested that we write letters-to-the-editor to local newspapers in support of the issues. This would give him the backing he needed to vote for arms control while representing a conservative state. After half an hour, John and I shook hands and agreed to stay in touch.

In the taxi to National Airport, I realized that I had flown quite high and my wings were still intact. Perhaps the messages of the lightning bolt and my dreams were right and I did not need to be so afraid. Yet I felt that I couldn't control the terror that rose up when I was faced with a new and unfamiliar task. I promised myself that I would do my best to assuage my fears by remembering the successes that were heaping up. I thought of a brave Joan of Arc who said, "I am not afraid... I was born to do this."

One Note.

I wrote one note to Aaron—a single note—and that note changed everything. I listened to Doug Flanders without reacting and invited him to tell me more, and that simple act opened the possibility of a relationship with Bill Boner.

Could it be that simple? I asked myself. *Could one kind act change everything?*

Other lobbyists experienced Aaron's crustiness and coolness as arrogance, unfriendliness, or hostility, and they were cool and crusty in return. They tried to badger him with counter proposals and counter arguments, or they decided he was not persuadable, clasped their briefcases to their chests, and walked out in a huff.

Some claimed that you could expect nothing else from a defense analyst working on Capitol Hill and thus used the excuse of Aaron's behavior—and Doug Landers'—to shore up their belief that politicians and their ilk were nothing but a cast of intractable, shoddy characters.

From Re-evaluation Counseling, I knew not to respond negatively. RC taught that every human being was essentially loving and infinitely intelligent, and that former hurts in ourselves and others were the only thing that kept us from seeing those qualities in another person. I knew that by acting on this assumption, it would allow the real human to shine through.

My commitment to build a long-term relationship with Al Gore was primary, but I also knew that I would stumble and fall if I discounted Aaron Wolfe, reacted timidly or hostilely, or crossed him off my list. It was clear to me that building a relationship with Gore required that I also build a relationship with Wolfe.

It was personally risky to believe I could build such relationships while maintaining my own integrity and the integrity of the ideas I represented on behalf of my friends in Tennessee. Without a clear sense of purpose, I might be sucked into the heady atmosphere of Capitol Hill; I might lose myself in the thrill of being close to those in positions of power.

Support from "the other side" continued to nudge me forward, however. I couldn't turn back with the voice of my dreams and the deft hand of Spirit guiding my steps. It might be scary and thrilling, but it was a risk I had to take.

4
Write to Me

Paul, Louise, and I organized a group of ten people to meet with Representative Bill Boner, just as Doug Landers had suggested. Among our group were grandmothers, parents, physicians, business owners, elementary school teachers, university students, and professors.

We planned the agenda: As we had done with Gore, we would introduce ourselves individually so that the congressman would know who we were and why we cared deeply about halting the nuclear arms race. Our hope was to show him that people from many segments of the community shared our concerns.

We would appreciate him for the things he had done to help people in our district, such as his votes to support services for senior citizens and people with physical handicaps. This would be a crucial part of the meeting. If we talked only about nuclear weapons, the conversation would be oppositional, since Rep. Boner had voted for every nuclear weapons system the Pentagon had proposed. Our hope was that by appreciating his other votes, we would set a tone of cordiality, signaling to him that we were not just another lobby group with a single-focused agenda.

Next, Paul would present our concerns about nuclear weapons and the legislation we hoped Boner would support. Finally, we would ask Boner to share his thoughts and feelings about the nuclear arms race. This would give us a chance to better understand the congressman's underlying assumptions and the motivation for his positions.

It would not be a typical lobby meeting with a member of Congress. More often, two or three people would present their position and what they wanted, and the congressman or his or her aide would counter by explaining his approach. Such meetings were usually cordial, but rarely did one leave with the feeling that anything would change.

We wished for a different result: improved communication between Rep. Boner and our group, and the possibility of further communication. Our ultimate goal was a change in his voting pattern, but we did not set a goal of changing his votes after just one meeting. It seemed more possible that this might happen over time. By introducing ourselves and asking him about his feelings regarding nuclear weapons, we hoped to open a door that until then had been boarded shut.

Since we did not represent the moneyed interests in Boner's district, but rather a range of "ordinary" people from different sectors of the community, it would do no good to try to pressure Boner. Instead, we hoped that our meeting would call on the representative's higher instincts—his inclination to do the right thing.

I called Boner's Nashville office to make an appointment. When I told the receptionist that there would be ten of us, she expressed surprise and said she would allot fifteen minutes on the congressman's busy schedule. She reminded me that it was two weeks before Christmas and the congressman had many things to attend to.

It was a brisk December morning when Bill Boner's aide ushered us into the congressman's office, where chairs formed a semicircle. Boner sat at his desk in a white shirt, dark pants, and red tie. A navy blue suit jacket hung on a coat rack near the door. The congressman rose to shake our hands.

Once seated, we introduced ourselves. "I'm a teacher and a grandmother," one woman said, "and I'm deeply worried about the future, for the sake of my grandchildren and for the children who have been my students." The man beside her added, "I'm a physician. My purpose is to save as many lives as I can, but my work will be fruitless if the world is destroyed in a nuclear holocaust." Boner listened and nodded after each person spoke, apparently surprised that we were doing this, but paying close attention.

"Congressman Boner." Boner's eyes shifted to focus on me. "We want to thank you for your efforts to support the citizens of Davidson County, especially your votes to help seniors, handicapped persons, teachers, and small business owners." In addition to our recognizing Boner for his efforts, mentioning his votes also showed that we were paying attention to his actions in Washington.

"Thank you, I appreciate that," Rep. Boner said.

Then Paul presented our concerns about the arms race, calling on Boner to support efforts to stop testing, producing, and deploying nuclear weapons. "Why do we need more weapons," Paul asked, "when we already have enough to blow up the world many times over?" Boner nodded slightly at Paul's points. "Also, Congressman, other interests of yours would benefit from the funds that are freed up."

Paul looked intently at Boner. "Congressman, we'd like to hear your thoughts and feelings about the nuclear arms race."

Boner glanced around the circle. "I just returned from a Pentagon-sponsored trip to Nebraska. Several other congressmen and I went to view the B-1 bomber installations. They took us underground to see the missiles in their silos." He paused and his voice jerked. "I was scared to look at them. I couldn't believe how big they were."

Paul nodded in agreement. "Yes, we understand they are huge."

"I was overcome with emotion. I didn't realize they were that enormous." Boner's voice was shaking. His eyes watered, and he choked back tears.

We sat quietly, our attention on Boner.

"You know, it's hard for me. I try hard to do what's right."

"Yes, of course," I said.

Bill Boner pulled forward a large corrugated box that sat

on the floor beside his desk and pushed it into the center of the circle of chairs. "You see this?"

We peered inside to a pile of perhaps a hundred envelopes addressed to the congressman.

"These are from my constituents. I read every letter I get. Write to me, and write 'Personal' on the envelope. I will read your letters and I'll respond."

"Thank you, Congressman," Paul said. "We appreciate this offer. We will definitely take you up on it."

We thanked Boner for his openness and his willingness to hear from us, then lined up to shake his hand before leaving his office. Our fifteen-minute meeting had stretched to an hour.

Over the next six months, Boner's voting record changed from 100% for nuclear weapons, to 50% for and 50% against. The change carried through the remainder of his time in Congress. These results far exceeded what we had hoped for from the meeting and pleased us very much. We suspected that he would continue to vote for legislation that funded weapons-related businesses in his district, because they gave money to his campaigns, but a change in half of his votes was a huge victory.

Would his votes have changed without the meeting? Doug Landers had said he listened to his constituents, so it was possible that the meeting had made a difference. We thought it a miracle that Boner had visited the Nebraska missile sites just prior to meeting with us. Was his visit by chance, I wondered, or guided by Spirit?

Dove Eggs.

In the political world of Washington, D.C., everyone has a demand. Lobbyists walk into congressional offices, often uninvited, selling their wares. Constituents back home call asking for help with a myriad of requests. Other members of

Congress push, pull, and coerce their colleagues to support their pet projects. And the White House bears down heavily, trying to push the president's legislative agenda. Who wouldn't end some days with a glazed look?

I expected that my efforts would take much longer to come to fruition, but in every case, with Spirit's presence and encouragement to act from a place of love—by listening, supporting, and asking key questions of everyone I met—changes occurred quickly.

After I'd been lobbying on Capitol Hill for several years, the *Washington Post* ran an interview with two prominent arms control lobbyists with forty years of experience between them. The interviewer asked them how many individual votes they thought they had changed. One person said "none," and the other said "maybe one or two." I was surprised by their answers, given either out of modesty or in truth. I wondered why they continued to do this work.

With Spirit's guidance, what I saw with my own eyes was that votes—and hearts—were changed.

5
An Exchange of Letters

In early February 1984, Peter and I talked about Gore's Senate campaign and the role of the local and statewide Freeze efforts. We discussed voter registration, as several Freeze activists would be involved in registering voters in poorer neighborhoods. Peter was interested in how this would relate to their campaign efforts, but was apparently unhappy with our plans. I got off the phone a little dissatisfied with how the conversation had ended.

I thought about what I wanted to say and called back the next day.

Peters laughed when he answered the phone. "Your ears must have been burning!"

"You were talking about me?"

"Yes," he said. "The problem with voter registration has been solved."

I teased him about being so speedy, then told him that I thought he was a fine person.

"The feeling is mutual," he said.

"I appreciate your cheerfulness and your patience in sorting out the issues with me."

"Likewise," Peter said. "It's my pleasure."

Paul Slentz, who was in Washington at the time, met with Peter and Aaron the following day. During their meeting, Aaron expressed an interest in exploring a ban on nuclear weapons testing, which was the first third of three parts of a total Freeze. I was pleasantly surprised. Aaron would look into the technical problems of banning all nuclear tests and also what form a test ban could take legislatively.

March 1984. I called Aaron at home after trying to reach him at his office all week. He was scheduled to arrive the following Friday to meet with our Freeze group, on what would be his first trip to Tennessee. I needed to confirm the details of his visit.

The conversation was cordial, but brief. Aaron was pleased that I'd called him at home and invited me to do so anytime. He said that Al was lucky to have me working with him.

Aaron had recently met with Chap Morrison, the legislative director of the Nuclear Weapons Freeze Campaign, for the first time. Aaron and Chap had talked genially, confidentially. Aaron shared his strategy approach with Chap and told Chap he thought that what the Freeze wanted would require "a revolution in consciousness." Aaron reasoned, therefore, that his own approach was more doable. I felt that my relationship with Aaron had opened the door to Aaron meeting with Chap.

The night before talking to Aaron, I'd had a dream in which I was walking down the street with a black man toward whom I felt warmly. We were going somewhere important. When I woke up I knew that the black man was Aaron. Jungian psychology would say that this black dream character represented my "shadow side," the source of masculine power within me, a positive image rather than a negative one. In many Eastern and shamanic cultures, black is viewed as the space out of which God created the heavens and the earth. It is the origin of everything, especially truth.

The dream about Aaron occurred in the context of a flurry of dreams about Gore himself. There had been ten since I wrote my first letter. The dreams showed Gore and me in frequent communication: attending meetings together, Al giving me papers to read, and seeing each other and waving from a distance. I believed that we were actually communicating on another level of reality, and that our communication in the dreams was as real as our communication in waking life. I had recorded the dreams about Al and Aaron since the first one, as they seemed to guide and inform me in a way I had not experienced before. They were a constant surprise, and I puzzled about why there were so many.

Two days before Aaron was to arrive in Nashville, Peter called. "I have bad news. Aaron has a conflict and won't be able to come."

I tried to hide my disappointment. I had looked forward to our Freeze group meeting with Aaron, feeling that it would help both sides better understand one another.

"I have good news, too." Peter laughed. "We're sending a replacement—Al himself!"

I laughed too. The group would be pleased. I knew it was in Al's best interest to meet with his constituents as often as he could and that perhaps he had orchestrated the change.

Washington Monthly had just named Gore one of the six best in Congress. "One of the most significant contributions a member of Congress can make is to investigate a problem and transform it into a legislative issue." The author cited the hearings in which Senator Kefauver exposed organized crime in the early fifties. "One of the best current practitioners of the art is another congressman from Tennessee," he wrote. "Representative Al Gore."

On Friday evening forty people gathered at the Catholic Center, our usual meeting place. Everyone took their seats and waited patiently for Gore's arrival. Half an hour past the appointed time, Gore strolled into the room, surrounded by aides. He took me aside to say he was between events and could stay for only an hour.

Then he leaned toward me and whispered, "Have I told this group about my dream?"

"Which dream?"

"About nuclear weapons."

I shook my head. "No, you haven't."

"Do you think it would be appropriate?"

I smiled and nodded. "Yes, it would. Please tell the dream."

With that, he handed his coat to an aide and whisked off to address the group.

Gore's dream had occurred two years earlier and had inspired his involvement in nuclear arms control. In the dream, a nuclear bomb exploded in the distance. Terrified, Gore looked down at a wrench in his hand and realized that it was of little use. He felt totally ill-prepared to help. When he awoke, he saw that he lacked the proper tools to deal with the nuclear threat and decided to learn everything he could about nuclear weapons so that he would be better equipped.

His dream, along with an experience of speaking to young women at Tennessee Girls State, had led him to contact Aaron Wolfe and request briefings on the nuclear arms race. At Girls State, Gore had asked the girls about their hopes for the future, to which they answered that they didn't think they would live to be adults. Deeply moved, he determined that he would become an expert on nuclear weapons, with the goal of reversing the arms race.

During his remarks to our group, Gore announced that he would sign onto a bill we were interested in and would consider joining us on a test ban. He suggested that we work together on several other arms control proposals.

His speech was greeted with loud applause. In the discussion that followed, several people referred to his dream and his Girls State experience, pleased that he was open to "other sources of information."

I saw immediately that Gore sharing his dream presented an opportunity to write him about mine, but I was afraid of how he might react. What would he say if I told him I thought he represented an aspect of myself that was becoming more powerful in the world, or that I felt certain he and I were communicating on another, nonmaterial, level?

After the meeting I started letters I was unable to finish, overcome by my fear about his reaction. Soon thereafter, there was another MX vote, and the ten-warhead missile system was kept alive by yet another compromise. Gore was instrumental in effecting the compromise. I was angry about his role in it, which made it even more difficult for me to write.

In April and May three more dreams about Gore flooded my consciousness. All three had a numinous quality. In one, we skated toward the Capitol building on icy sidewalks, effortlessly navigating a challenging and dangerous route to the power center of the nation. In another, we stood on opposite sides of the reflecting pool on Capitol Mall under a black sky, the stars glimmering above. This dream had an aura of peace and rightness about it and seemed to assert that the complement of our opposite stances brought balance and wholeness. In the third dream, we stood under water that poured over us to "enlighten" us, allowing us to see into the minds of others in Congress and into the future. These dreams awed me. They were blossoms on the vine of our developing relationship, messages about the flowering of our work together.

On May 30, 1984, Rep. Albert Gore, Jr., announced his candidacy for U.S. Senate. On that date there was also an eclipse of the sun. In astrology, a solar eclipse underlines whatever is going on at the time, adding emphasis to the day's events. The day seemed auspicious, indeed.

Louise and I drove to Gore's Nashville headquarters on Murphreesboro Road for the announcement. Gore's speech highlighted his 98% voting record in Congress and attendance at over 1,200 town meetings back home in Tennessee—an average of four meetings per week for every week he'd been in Congress, more than any other congressional representative. Numerous bills had originated from those town meetings, bills about infant formula, organ transplants, and the clean-up of hazardous wastes and chemical spills. He had led investigations that exposed a foreign-dominated uranium cartel responsible for a billion dollars in illegal overcharges in electric bills. The result was lower electric bills for consumers. Gore was proud of his record and told the audience that he was committed to holding town meetings in all ninety-five Tennessee counties on a regular basis if elected senator. Those listening to Gore tout his record were clearly excited.

I joined the caravan heading to the nearby airport for Gore's launch of a rash of statewide appearances. Before he boarded the plane, supporters lined up to wish him well, I among them.

He was flushed with excitement, his cheeks crimson. He beamed when he saw me. "I spoke on the House floor last week against testing anti-satellite weapons. I think you'll be pleased when you read it. My speech influenced the vote. I'll have Peter send you a copy."

I congratulated him on the speech and his announcement for Senate. "Thank you," I said. "I'd love to see it."

He smiled proudly, then turned to the person behind me. Before departing, he paused on the steps of the small plane that would take him to Memphis, as though acknowledging the significance of this historic moment. I felt it, too. It seemed certain he would be elected senator, and perhaps president after that.

The next day as I was leaving for the grocery store, I spotted my cat Holly sunning herself on a front window ledge. "Hey, Holly," I said, locking the door. She lifted her head and opened her eyes briefly, then closed them again. Holly was a long-haired calico with a sweet and fragile temperament. As I got into the car, an image of her being dragged off the ledge flickered through my mind, an image that barely registered.

The store was unusually busy and shopping took longer than usual. When I returned, Holly was not on the ledge. I figured she was under the bushes out back, as she got quite hot in the sun. Once I had put the groceries away and started the laundry, I went to the back door to call her. Holly didn't come, but it wasn't unusual for her to hide out for two or three hours.

After the laundry finished I decided to go looking. I circled the outside of the house and checked the garage. After several minutes of searching, I spotted her in a neighbor's backyard. I ran to where she lay and touched her. She was limp and cold, her neck bloodied. It appeared that a neighborhood dog had dragged her off the ledge and killed her. I stared in shock, kneeling beside her body for several minutes. Lifting her in my arms, I carried her through the backyards to a redwood bench on our patio, where I wrapped her in a towel and watched over her until Ron could get home from work.

We cried and buried her under a bush near the garage. We would mourn her loss for several months. My premonition was such a fleeting thing, but I was upset with myself. Why hadn't I taken her inside?

I thought about Golda Meir in her days as Prime Minister of Israel, prior to the 1973 Yom Kippur War. Reports had reached Meir and her cabinet that Egypt and Syria were amassing troops on Israel's border. Meir's instinct was to prepare for war, but she wanted to hear from her cabinet. She went from person to person, asking their opinion. The twenty-nine-member, all-male cabinet believed, to a man, that Israel's mobilization was unnecessary and might in fact provoke a conflagration. Meir acquiesced reluctantly. Though she was fearful of an attack, she could not see going against the advice of her cabinet.

On October 6, the night before Yom Kippur, the Prime Minister was awakened in the night by a call informing her that Egypt and Jordan would attack Israel's border towns within twenty-four hours. Because Israel was not prepared, and because it would be impossible to mobilize on Yom Kippur, thousands of innocent Israeli citizens would be killed. Meir was stunned. When she hung up the telephone, she dropped her head into her hands and cried, "My God, why didn't I follow my intuition?"

I felt exactly like that. Why hadn't I put Holly in the house?

One of the phrases used in Re-evaluation Counseling as a counseling direction was, "Trust your own thinking, trust your own thinking, trust your own thinking." I had worked with this direction often, using it to inspire my telephone calls and letters to Gore and his staff. Now I saw how not writing to Gore about my dreams could be a retreat. My fear told me it would be a mistake to tell him, because dreams were so outside the context of Washington politics, but my heart urged me on. There was a strong nudging that wouldn't let me rest.

Finally I sat down to write. But before I could talk about the dreams, I needed to express my anger about his role vis-à-vis the MX missile, as well as about an article that had appeared in a Nashville newspaper calling Gore a "Reagan man."

May 28, 1984

Dear Al,

This is the third letter I've begun since your visit here in mid-March. I started to write and thank you for meeting with us, but there was more to say—reflections on the dream you shared with us, and on some of my own dreams—and I postponed finishing it. Then, after the MX vote, I found myself angrier than I expected, and a second draft was also set aside.

The MX vote reinforces for many the feeling that we are powerless in relation to a small group in Washington. The vote preempted an effort by a million or more people to kill the MX outright. We are frustrated that the vote occurred without our input.

I think that the most valuable gifts a politician can offer are listening (a skill you possess), a sense of hope about the future, and recognition and support for people taking charge of their lives. One way to do this is to translate people's concerns into legislation, which you've done well in areas such as health and safety, but which is not happening in the arena of arms control.

The enclosed article also displeased many. Some want to know why we should help elect you if those who vote for you might also vote for Reagan. It appears from the article that you think Reagan will be re-elected and that you wouldn't mind riding on his coattails. Does the article fairly represent what you think and feel?

Thank you for your offer to send a copy of your speech on the anti-satellite testing moratorium. I was moved by your testimony in committee, which Peter sent me earlier.

The public sharing of your dream at our March meeting was

important for many. It showed that you are open to listening to a variety of sources. I do believe that dreams are sources of information about ourselves, our relationships, and problems in our external world—and sometimes they are also "visits" with people in our lives, communication that has not been realized on an external level.

I say this because you have appeared in my dreams often in the last year. The dreams are so strongly in my consciousness as I sit down to write, that the alternative seems to be to write nothing at all. About a month ago the words came to me, "I wish I could tell Al Gore the truth." It is this that motivates me to tell you now. While I do not wish to inflate their significance, I know that they are important to me, and it is possible that the messages will have meaning for you. There have been thirteen that I can remember.

- Many have enacted a communication between us: a wave from afar, an exchange of information, a conversation.
- Almost all have been about our work. We have attended meetings together and talked with groups of people; you have given speeches and announced your candidacy.
- There have been many positive images. In one, we stood under streams of water that allowed us access into the minds of people in Congress and knowledge of the future. In another, we stood on opposite sides of the reflecting pool in Washington and "knew" everything was right.

What I understand from these dreams is this: (1) Perhaps there is something we will accomplish together; (2) You represent a part of me that is flourishing—your clear thinking and effective action, the "masculine" qualities. In one dream you sat and listened to women, which led me to wonder if you are also integrating feminine qualities of warmth, listening, and nurturing more effectively; (3) Communication may be happening at another, more spiritual level; (4) Despite our opposing viewpoints, our work together is positive and on the right track.

I have not wanted to impose on you my sense of our connection. But I've also realized that you may intuit some of what I've said here, and that my being explicit may be helpful. I treasure our friendship and wish you the best as you embark on your election campaign.

Caroline

I held my breath for the next few days, waiting for a shoe to drop. I was afraid my letter would undercut the work I had done to build relationships with Gore and Wolfe; that Gore would decide to distance himself from me in the future.

At the end of the week, I received a small ivory envelope addressed in Gore's own hand. In the upper left corner were the words "U.S. House of Representatives." In the upper right corner was Gore's preprinted signature: Albert Gore, Jr., M.C. (Member of Congress)

I sat down on the couch to open the envelope. Inside was a handwritten note:

Dear Caroline,

Thank you for your gentle and heartwarming letter. I, too, treasure our friendship and believe there is much good we can do together.

I understand your anger about the MX compromise (now modified further, of course), but you shouldn't feel any concern about the article. I will be working to defeat Reagan and elect the Democratic nominee (Mondale, I assume). However, there will be many Tennesseans who vote for both me and Reagan. Am I supposed to tell them not to, or make it hard for them? I want to make it easy for them, while at the same time encouraging those who are persuadable to vote for Mondale.

I will send you the debates on ASAT [anti-satellite weapons] and SLCM [sea-launched cruise missiles]. Both were great victories for arms control. There is now a chance they will be preserved in the conference committee, and that fifteen MXs will be the cost. The Freeze folks here will acknowledge privately that this is a good result, but the symbolism of the MX is such that they will never say so publicly. And they probably shouldn't.

In any event, I look forward to working with you and learning.

Sincerely,
Al

I was pleased with his efforts for arms control, although hardly persuaded that fifteen MX missiles with their 150 warheads was a good result. The multi-billion-dollar MX was much more than a symbol! However, I thought it was a miracle that he was open to hearing about my dreams and that he looked forward to working with me "and learning." That he had taken the time to write in his own hand indicated he understood the risk I had taken. I breathed a sigh of relief.

To my utter and complete amazement, once I received Al's note, the frequency of the dreams increased. During the next two months, I had five more dreams about Al and one about Aaron.

I was baffled by this turn of events. I had thought that telling Al about the dreams would let the air out of my hot air balloon so that I, the dreamer, could return to earth. Instead, it seemed that I had thrown the ballast overboard, for the balloon was lifted on the currents, propelled higher and more rapidly now, toward some faraway, unknown shore. I was floating over uncharted territory at the mercy of the winds of destiny.

The Night Wind.

Was there a purpose in these dreams—this continued other worldly communication that I had received for over a year—a purpose beyond what I already understood?

I had looked deeply at the dreams with my friend Linda Odom, a psychologist and student of dream analysis. I understood the roles that Al and Aaron were playing in my inner life as *animus* and *shadow*, aspects of the personality described by Carl Jung. As well, I believed that all dreams visit us in the service of health and wholeness, and that no dream comes simply to tell the dreamer what he or she already knows.

I also believed that there might be an actual communication with Al that occurred in the dream state, as well as the possibility of messages intended for him. Many men, including those in the world of politics, live in their minds, too caught up in mental activity to tune into such messages. Their mental world keeps them from being open to Spirit as it blows through their lives. It seemed that the night wind carried dream messages to me as a means of tying our destinies together.

I was grateful that Al had not closed a door on my sharing the dreams I received. He had responded kindly, gently, and expressed an interest in continuing to learn more. He had opened the door to internal counsel—from himself, I felt sure, as well as what came from me.

I couldn't change the dreams nor force them to go away. I wasn't choosing the dreams; they were choosing me. I could only surrender to their presence and hope to understand what they had come to say.

6
Love Aaron

In July 1984, five years after my sister Cathy's death, Al Gore's sister, Nancy, died of lung cancer. Reading about Nancy and her life, I was struck by similarities in our sisters' deaths. Both Al and I had just one sibling each, a sister, and both died of cancer when we were thirty-six years old. Both of their lives were cut short because of exposure to toxic chemicals.

I wrote him a note of condolence and told him about the book I was writing that described the spiritual experiences I had had around Cathy's death. With the note I included a copy of a poem called "After Winter" that I had written when Cathy died. Although I wrote the poem for Cathy, I felt that the poem actually contained her words of comfort for me. Al penned a note in return, saying that the poem was beautiful and that he welcomed the opportunity to read my book.

Then a whirlwind danced into our lives, Ron's and mine—two whirlwinds, to be exact. Earlier in the year we had applied to adopt two Korean children. We received notice, along with photos of a brother and sister, Yang So Suk and Yang Jung Hwa, that they would arrive at the Nashville airport on July 24. We decided to name them David and Amy, which mean "beloved" in Hebrew and French, and to maintain Yang, their Korean last name, as their middle name. New friends of ours and their two adopted Korean children joined us to welcome David and Amy at the airport.

David and Amy were sweet and adorable and spoke no English. They had the energy of any six- and seven-year-olds.

They played the piano and guitar and sang Korean nursery rhymes. In the bath, singing and chattering, they scrubbed themselves heartily with washcloths, a habit developed in the orphanage. We had been advised that it could take a long while for them to accept us as their parents, but on the second day, when Ron returned home from work, David called him Daddy. Despite warnings we had received to the contrary—as in "don't get your hopes up"—they were immediately affectionate and loved their new home. Their arrival was happy and exciting, and a major adjustment for all four of us.

Through the late summer and early fall I directed a voter registration drive in preparation for the elections. As predicted, Gore was elected to the Senate by a landslide, and Ronald Reagan was re-elected to the White House. This was the same Ronald Reagan who had called the Soviet Union "the evil empire" and who had refused to consider any form of arms control. Reagan's re-election was a depressing event in the lives of those who had worked hard to elect someone who might take a Freeze seriously. My friends in the Freeze campaign were disheartened and demoralized.

I was exhausted from the election campaign and the changes in our family life. My neck continued to hurt from the lightning bolt, and I had no idea why. Hadn't I heeded its directives? Hadn't I written that first letter and continued to work on building a relationship with Al Gore? Was there something I hadn't done yet, some message I'd failed to understand?

A friend recommended a sojourn at Kripalu Yoga and Health Center in western Massachusetts as a way to nurture myself and rejuvenate. I agreed to make the trek. The week between Christmas and New Year's, I joined fifty others to meditate, do yoga postures, soak in a hot tub, and walk in the Massachusetts woods. The food was macrobiotic and grown fresh on the grounds, the healthiest and best-tasting food I'd ever eaten.

Our workshop leaders talked about the energy that flows through the human body and exists in all things. It was a new concept for me, and although I had been introduced to yoga a decade earlier, this type of yoga had a different focus; namely, opening up the energy centers in the body. We did an activity where we focused on feeling energy in our hands. During the exercise, the leader directed us to place our hands on a part of our body that needed healing. My hands automatically went to my neck.

To my amazement, the pain went away. "What happened?" I asked afterward, incredulous.

The leader explained how a powerful energy flows through the palms of the hands that can be directed toward healing. The energy releases points of tension and brings balance to the muscles, bones, and organs. I was told that I could schedule an "energy balancing" session with a body worker for a small fee, which I immediately signed up for. During the session, the pain again left my neck and shoulders completely.

When I asked the resident physician about these experiences, he told me they indicated that the pain in my neck resided in the subtle energy fields of the body. He said that I had the energy of a twenty-year-old, even though I was nearly forty years old, and by taking care of myself in this particular way, I would feel that energy again.

I returned home optimistic that my neck would heal, although the healing process seemed very slow. There were brief periods without pain, but it always returned. With the election behind us, I immersed myself once more in writing the book about my sister.

One afternoon while writing, I became aware of a screen in my mind upon which flashed "yes" and "no" answers. Once I became aware of the screen, I realized that I had unconsciously relied on this screen for over a year.

I decided to test it out. Should I go home by way of 18th Avenue? *No.* Should I go home by way of 12th Avenue? *Yes.* I followed these directions, only later to find out that there had been an accident on 18th Avenue.

Is this a good time to call my mother? *No.* I waited half an hour. Okay, is this a good time to call my mother? *Yes.* When I called, she told me she had just returned from the grocery store.

The answers were always correct. They resolved questions about my everyday life, interpreted my dreams, and made suggestions about a whole range of activities and people. Unconsciously I had been using the screen to tell me when to call Peter, Aaron, and Al Gore; when to contact Rep. Boner's and Sen. Sasser's offices; when to write my letters; what to include in the letters. Was it a good idea to tell them I was planning to come to Washington? *Yes.* Should I mention the build-down proposal? *No.*

I was startled by this discovery and wondered where this wisdom came from. Was it my "higher self" speaking? A heightened intuition that was working on my behalf? Or God/Spirit working on behalf of the nation and the world? Was it all three?

Religious texts are full of stories of God talking to those who are ready to listen. Angels, archangels, prophets, Jesus, Krishna, Shiva, and God have appeared to hundreds of individuals, offering solace, wisdom, and rebuke. It seemed presumptuous to think I was one of these, but I didn't have an answer for why I was receiving such guidance.

I had read several of the *Seth* books channeled by Jane Roberts in the 1960s and 1970s; *The Starseed Transmissions,* channeled by Ken Carey; and *Emmanuel,* transcribed by Pat Rodegast. At the time I became aware of the screen, I knew of few other channeled books. I wondered if this same phenomenon could be happening to me, and if so, whose voice this was.

One day I asked the screen whether I was doing the right things to heal my neck, and the screen answered *no.*

The thought that I was not doing enough made me angry. Since my visit to Kripalu, I had done yoga every morning, had changed my diet, and was seeing a chiropractor twice a week. This was all that I knew to do.

I responded in frustration, "What do you mean, 'no'? I don't know what else to do."

The answer came back: *We thought you'd never ask.*

This took my breath away, and I sat for a few minutes pondering the existence of a voice. A dialog began in my head between what I thought was my own mind and this voice. Finally, I took out a pen and began to write: "Who are you?"

We've been with you all along. We are the source of true information.

I considered this possibility. "Am I making this up?" I wrote.

No, you are not.

I was willing to see where this led. "I've been doing everything I know to heal my neck but nothing seems to help. What do I need to do? Please help."

A voice spoke inside my mind, which I transcribed: *We have two pieces of advice. First, slow down and smell the flowers. You are pushing too hard, trying to make things work. The flowers are always there, just as we are always here. Take the time to notice. Slow down enough so that you can fully enjoy present time.*

This seemed wise advice, but not earth-shattering. At the time, I didn't realize how valuable this advice was for me.

"And the second?"

The second is to love Aaron.

"Love Aaron?"

This suggestion baffled me. I was married with a family, as was he. I wasn't into extramarital affairs. What could they possibly mean?

Yes, love Aaron. Simply that.

Voices.

The Bible, the Torah, the Koran, the Vedas, and many other religious texts purport to have been passed from God to humans. Without humans hearing the voice of God, no religious texts would exist. All are the result of humans writing down what they hear, whether from a burning bush, the blaring of trumpets, a visit from an angel, or a voice in the head.

The inspired truth of Spirit requires that someone write or speak on its behalf. It communicates to those with a certain spiritual openness, ready to hear. What other way is there to receive the truth? As far as I know, God doesn't write, whether in Sanskrit, English, Arabic, or Greek.

In 21st century America, tens of millions of people have read books containing conversations with God and messages from angels. In 1984, few would have believed me if I'd said that Spirit was directing my actions on Capitol Hill through words I transcribed onto paper.

I was amazed by the appearance of voices and puzzled by their existence, yet I felt in the fibers of my being that these were voices of truth. Their directive to love Aaron was a mystery to me. It was a bold request, beyond anything I could have conceived on my own, definitely outside the cultural norms. I knew this was not about forming a romantic or physical relationship. Still, it felt terribly risky, especially if I were to play a role in ending the nuclear arms race. What would it mean to love him beyond what I had already done? And how would this heal my neck?

Yet I was being asked to do this thing. Why else should I take such a risk?

7
Love Is the Truth

In mid-December, Peter flew to Nashville to confer with Gore's Tennessee staff. He and I met over lunch to discuss Freeze Campaign objectives and Gore's arms control proposals. As always, Peter was cordial and upbeat. I told him the Nashville Peace Alliance would like to have a meeting with Gore to discuss several arms control issues. Peter suggested March, after Gore returned from the arms control talks in Geneva.

All appeared to be flowing smoothly, yet beneath the surface the waters seemed muddied. One day I was perfectly clear about what I was doing; the next, I felt terribly confused. In a moment of frustration, I pleaded with God, the voices, and whoever else could hear me: "I wish to be of service, but I don't know what I need to do. Please help."

Words came, which I wrote down:

Give us expression in all the places you go. Love people everywhere. You are ready for this. Begin now. There is no need to plan or worry about the future. The future takes care of itself.

Please be specific. What are you asking me to do with regard to my disarmament work?

Sit in silence before each phone call and each letter you write. Sit until you feel love for the person you are calling or writing.

I was doing this much of the time and resolved to do this on every occasion. When I had asked the voices about healing my neck, they told me to love Aaron. "Okay," I wrote. "Why Aaron, in particular?"

First, as with Gore, you have important work to accomplish

78

together. You need do no more than feel love in your heart before you interact with him. You have also known him in past lifetimes—in Egypt, Syria, and Eastern Europe. In Eastern Europe, you were on the run together, hiding from authorities. This experience gives you the feeling that you already know him well.

This realm of Spirit was full of surprises. I had not expected this answer. Yet the concept of past lives was not foreign to me. When I was twenty-five, I had opened a magazine to a two-page spread of a lush mountain scene that I recognized immediately. I had shown it to a friend and told her the scene was in Nepal, northwest of Kathmandu. I'd never seen photos of Nepal, but the caption on the next page confirmed my knowing. The only explanation that made sense to me was that I had been there in another life. Since then, images and stories had offered themselves when I wanted to understand an especially deep connection I felt to someone, or why a place seemed overly familiar. These scenarios had helped me make sense of situations and feelings I could not otherwise explain.

Ron was fascinated by the guides telling me about past life experiences and suggested that I visit a coworker of his who on weekends saw clients as a psychic. I was not one to run to psychics to solve my problems, so I had mixed feelings about calling her, but in the end I decided to go, hoping she could offer wisdom that would help heal my neck.

Juanita lived in a small suburban house in Smyrna, southeast of Nashville. A slight, dark-haired woman in her forties, she led me to the kitchen and indicated a chair at her kitchen table, then sat down across from me and began to talk. Her comments were wide-ranging, touching on my health, my family, and my spiritual life. Some of what she said was accurate; some not. Although I did not mention Gore by name, Juanita told me I had had three past lives with him. When I asked her to comment about Aaron, she said, "He can be difficult to work with." After my first meeting with Aaron, I had not found this to be true. Later the voices told me that she had picked up on his "usual way of being."

On the drive home I wondered if it were true that I had had

past lives with both Al and Aaron. Certainly the connections were strong, but was this why? In the car I felt the voices nudging me, as though they were eager to speak.

In the cool of my living room, I took out pen and paper.

You are here, they said, which was how they began these dialogs, as though *they* were always here, and it was I who was only sometimes present.

I spoke to them: "I continue to act out of love in my relationships as best I can, but I'm unclear about my next steps."

We applaud your efforts. Keep it up. We're proud of you for not denying the truth of love.

"Tell me about Juanita's comments. Several of them seem off-track."

Some are possible futures; others are probable futures. But you don't need Juanita right now. You're doing fine on your own.

"What is my karmic debt to Al?"

It isn't what you expect.

"Will you tell me?"

Only part of it now. What you need to know is this: In the most recent life, on the plains of Wyoming, you were like a fawn, a treasure, a delicate thing in his life, which life was otherwise rough and difficult, full of death and destruction. He was a killer then.

"And I?"

An innocent child. A sweet girl. Very young. You represented to him the purity of life. You were his sanity, his bridge to the truth of life.

"Then why and what do I owe him?"

He saved your life while killing others, including your family. You were plunder, the enemy's loot. He lifted you onto his horse and carried you away.

In the life before that one, he gunned you down. You were his brother, and he saw too late the love in your eyes.

"If this is true, then it seems that *he* owes *me* something."

Not quite. In still an earlier life, your laws, the laws of ancient Egypt, killed him. He became a sacrifice to your legal system, and you didn't bat an eye.

"These lives all revolve around giving and taking life."

Yes, it's true. In the most recent life, when he saved you, you developed a debt of gratitude and a tenderness toward him that propels you now.

"Am I making this up? How can I know if it's real?"

The karmic tie is very deep, very tight. Only his saving your life explains it. Now you are intent on saving his.

"How can I do this? It sounds impossible to me."

We can't tell you this. But we will say that loving him will never be a mistake. Nothing will be lost and much gained. Love him defensively, in an attitude of protection. He needs your help.

Soon I identified the voices in my head as spirit guides, emissaries of God or Spirit. When asked, they told me they were five. The voices repeatedly urged me to love Gore, Wolfe, Sasser, Boner, members of my family, and others. I struggled to follow their guidance. I co-counseled with Louise, clearing away the fear that arose when I was asked to take a new step or when the responses from others were not positive. My friend Linda and I also met weekly to share and study our dreams.

Like water coursing downstream, many dreams flowed through my consciousness during this time: dreams of "dressing for the job"; of persuading members of Congress to vote a certain way; of Al observing me in churches and other holy sites, as though he hoped to learn how I integrated spirituality into my life.

In one dream, Aaron was counting on me to help make his case before a congressional committee, but I left the committee meeting early. I didn't realize until afterwards that he had needed me and that I could have been of help. When I awoke, I wondered if it were true that he needed me to help in some way.

On February 24, 1985, I dreamed that I decided to apply for a job. The interview took place at the Bethlehem Center, an actual community center in North Nashville. Three men were sitting in the front room to interview me. After the interview, a woman named Mary shook my hand and offered me the job.

The Bethlehem Center, three wise men, and Mary—I could almost smell frankincense and myrrh! I understood this symbolism as a direct message from Spirit.

The previous day I had learned that the position of director of Common Cause-Tennessee was open, a statewide organizing job that included lobbying at the state legislature. I had taken up writing again and had no intention of taking a job, but from the dream I knew that I must apply, and that the job would be mine.

I called about the position that morning. The hiring committee interviewed me at 2:00 p.m. and hired me to start in three days.

In early March, Peter told me that Gore was counting on President Reagan to keep his promise that the MX would be a bargaining chip with the Soviets, i.e., that the MX would never actually be built. It would serve solely as a threat to induce the Soviets to give up some of their existing weapons in negotiations. Publicly, Reagan was saying that he intended to go forward with the new system. One of my dreams predicted this latter result.

I wrote Gore a letter that would be waiting for him when he returned from Geneva. I mentioned Reagan's promise and asked Gore what encouraged him to believe that the president would keep his word. I then tackled the issue of fear:

… I have thought often about your analysis of fear: the kernel of reality surrounded by a cloud of illusion. You have equated the predominant fear of the peace movement (the proliferation of nuclear weapons) with the predominant fear of the Reagan administration (the Soviets), treating them pretty much the same. For a long time I've thought there was a difference between the two, although I have not been able to articulate the difference. Two nights ago, an answer came in a dream:

I am sitting in a train car with my husband Ron, a woman

friend, and a man I hardly know. The woman and man are in the peace movement but don't know each other. The car sits on a beautiful grassy meadow. Across a valley to a nearby hill are two black-and-white boats in which we have flown to arrive at this place. I turn to my companions and ask, "How are the fears different?"

Suddenly army planes and tanks appear on the hill. They have seen the boats and believe we are dangerous intruders. The man and woman run at full speed down a road that extends from the train car. I tell them to keep low so they can't be seen, but because of their fear, they do not. Ron and I crawl slowly behind them. But the other couple in their unthinking fear has given us away, and the army comes to kill all of us. I am the first to be caught—at a crossroads.

Here is what I understand: The dream is about the integration of black and white, male and female—what is needed in order to end the arms race. It recalls my first letter to you, where I spoke about racism and sexism being the roots of the arms race. Masculine qualities of rationality, assertiveness, and aggression are running our country, almost entirely absent the more feminine qualities of nurturance, relationship, intuition, and listening to one's inner truth.

The peace movement's fear of nuclear war endangers us only because the weapons and the armies exist. The armies with their weapons endanger us all. One fear calls for more weapons; the other calls for fewer weapons. Without the weapons, there is no real danger. The army and the unrelated masculine/feminine fear each other. Fearing the other, we endanger ourselves and everyone else. We have to give up fearing the other and view others as part of ourselves. This includes how we view the Soviets.

I appreciate your efforts to lessen U.S. and Soviet fears of each other and urge you to continue to focus on this. I encourage you, while not giving up your thoughtful analysis, to listen more and more to your own heart.

On another note, I became Executive Director of Common Cause/ Tennessee on March 1st and will now wear another hat in relation to you and your staff. I am coming to Washington April 2-4 for orientation and will make an appointment with you or Aaron.

Aaron mentioned that you wish to devise a national public education strategy on space weapons. In Nashville we have had three public meetings on this topic. We are very interested in public education about the arms race and wish to be of help in any way we can.

Sincerely,
Caroline

Indeed, I *was* at a crossroads. I was constantly being called to stand up for what I believed to be the truth—spiritually, morally, and politically. I could either take the easy way and back down from the life that lay before me, or I could listen to the voice of Spirit and act on the basis of what I was told.

I was being called to continue to build the relationships with Gore and Wolfe without knowing where this would lead, and to do it with love—a deep unconditional love. It seemed a paradox, and I knew others would perceive it in this way. I was being asked to love deeply those I disagreed with politically, to honor the voices and stories of past lives, and to maintain my values and perspectives without seeking cover. It was my task to stand at the crossroads between the world of politics and the voice of Spirit calling me to love—to stand and allow the world to see what I was doing. It felt dangerous and risky, as though my life were on the line, even though some part of me knew that love was the truth.

When I was a student at California Lutheran College, I had attended daily chapel. One morning, as the guest speaker talked about the Christian life, his voice became louder, exhorting us to understand some key point. He started walking around the seventy-five of us who sat in the audience, continuing to raise his voice. Suddenly he stopped and yelled, "When I say 'stand up,' stand up!" At that point, every person in the room stood up, except me. He came to where I sat and yelled again, "When I say 'stand up,' stand up!" I refused to stand.

Then he asked everyone to sit down. He told us that we (this group) should not have stood up at his command. That we needed to think for ourselves. That there was no reason to stand, no reason to obey his command. He reminded us about Adolf Hitler and those who followed him. He told us we must be strong within ourselves and honor that which we knew to be true.

He must have been surprised that I remained seated because he never mentioned the fact that one person had disobeyed him, that I alone had listened to myself. I had sat in my truth, knowing not to follow blindly. Remaining seated strengthened my moral fiber. I carried this incident into my life as a reminder to follow my inner moral compass.

I thought now about the choices that faced me. Would I continue to follow the guidance I was being given, that spoke to me in my heart? Or would I choose to ignore this gift? And if so, why would I ignore it? Because I was afraid? The gift was leading me to a life of greater love and integrity, a life of deeper meaning.

I turned to the voices for guidance: "Do you know everything I need to know?"

Yes, ask us what you like.

"Am I doing the right thing by focusing on loving these men?"

Of course.

"It's scary."

Of course.

"Will they recognize it?"

Not always. But they will learn to trust it. We are leading you down this path for a purpose. The purpose—ending the nuclear arms race—is indeed connected to the truth of love.

I called Peter to go over last-minute details for the meeting with Gore. While waiting for him to pick up the line. I thought, "He's going to say, 'You sure know when people are thinking about you, don't you?'"

Peter's voice came on the phone. "Do you have ESP or something? I've just been trying to reach you."

"Yes, I do." I laughed.

On March 22, Gore met with the Peace Alliance to discuss items that both he and we had placed on the agenda: the talks in Geneva, conflicts in Nicaragua and El Salvador, how to strengthen the U.N. for dealing with conflicts, the Space Defense Initiative (SDI) known as Star Wars, and a ban on nuclear test explosions.

Those who attended commented afterward that they felt Gore had heard their concerns and answered their questions. For me it was the process that felt rewarding: the preparations with Peter, the letter I had written to Gore, the relationship we were cultivating with our senator.

As for the MX missile, Gore's trust was betrayed. President Reagan pushed forward to develop the missiles, despite his promise to Gore.

From my new post near Legislative Plaza, I worked on building relationships with state legislators and their staffs while advocating for Common Cause's agenda. Two brief conversations with the Tennessee Speaker of the House led to a change in his vote, which made possible the passage of state legislation supporting an amendment to the U.S. constitution that had been languishing in the legislature for years. It seemed an easy victory.

I continued to follow Spirit's guidance, despite my feelings about the risks involved. In time I discovered the voices were always right; they never led me astray. Nevertheless, when they told me to love the people I worked with ever more deeply, I thought they were crazy, as though they wanted me to dive into the deepest part of the ocean. Not only was I to love these men, but I was to tell them how I felt! My mind said this was outrageous, crazy, and beyond reason.

During this time the guides told me repeatedly to love Aaron, to tell him how I felt, and not to retreat. I thought about how I could do this without becoming romantically entangled. After much thought, I decided to ask him if we could be friends. That seemed like a step I could reasonably take.

I would talk to Aaron on my upcoming trip to Washington, but the fear of taking yet another leap into the unknown was almost crippling. I hesitated to call him to request extra time for our meeting.

The guides spoke: *If you wait, it is less likely you will have the time you need.*

"If I were to call him, what could I say? It seems like such a straightforward task, but it feels incredibly difficult."

Ah, we see your fear! It is like a deep blue light hanging over your shoulders. Say to him, "Aaron, I've told you I want to spend some time with you. I want to tell you why."

How embarrassingly simple.

On April 1, the night before my flight to D.C., I had a dream in which Al came to speak to our group.

Gore and I stand in front of a group where I am the moderator. I feel a mild tension between the group and Gore. Then I leave and come back while he is still talking. I am impressed by the change in tone to one of cordiality.

In another meeting, a female staff person says that a national poll has found that people everywhere like Gore. She is pleased. I feel I haven't been cordial enough to him. I had pulled back because I was worried about being too cordial.

Everything goes black, and a voice says, "There is a death somewhere."

The scene changes. I go to a woman's house to offer comfort. On the way I see three dead male children being carried on boards by their fathers.

The scene changes again, and I am at a meeting where Gore is speaking and I am the moderator.

The notion of being too cordial to Gore resonated with me; some people had been saying I was too nice to him. Hearing this thought, the guides said, *Bah, humbug. You know we disagree.*

The dream was telling me that the guides were right. Perhaps one could not be too cordial.

I pondered the images of dead children and "a death somewhere." Was something in me dying—perhaps my old way of being in the world, fearful and uncertain of myself? I went through my journals. There had been thirty-nine dreams about Gore in two years. I wondered whether to tell him about the recent dreams, or if by doing so I would overwhelm him or worry him.

I set the journals aside in order to pack for my trip to D.C. I had asked both Al and Aaron for appointments. In fact, over the course of three days I had two meetings each with Peter and Aaron, and one with Al.

My first meeting with Aaron was about arms control. Before we parted, I asked if he thought we could rid the world of nuclear weapons using his approach. Did he see that as a desirable and feasible goal? Was it possible to get there?

He was silent for a few moments, mulling it over. "It may be possible."

He knew I had something more on my mind, so we agreed to meet at the entrance to the cafeteria on the last day of my visit.

On Thursday we found a table and settled into an uncomfortable silence.

Aaron sipped his coffee. "I want you to know that no matter what you say or have said to me previously, we can always have the relationship we have already. That is not in jeopardy."

"For me, too," I said. "I would never intentionally do anything to jeopardize our relationship."

He waited.

"Aaron, I know that you are very smart, very perceptive. It is something I like about you very much."

"If you believe that I'm smart, then know that I will understand what you say to me."

Okay, then. I took a breath. "I would like to be friends, although I don't know exactly what that would mean."

"Friends?" His brow furrowed. "Why would you want

to be friends with *me*? I keep feeling you'll find out what I'm really like, and you'll back off. I'm just a plain man, an ordinary man."

"When we met, remember the barbs you sent my way? And I liked you anyway? You've told me you kick the dog." He smiled at this. "This is of no consequence to me."

"I'm a hawk sometimes."

"That's funny." I'd known this from day one. "You don't think I know you're a hawk?"

This got a laugh out of him.

"I'm very flattered." He was turning his cup slowly. Then he looked up. "I'm more flattered by your approach than by anything in years. People don't often say these things to each other, give each other a gold star. I feel like you've just given me a gold star." His expression was warm, kind. "Then there's the matter of time—my time."

"I'm not asking for more of your time. I'm happy to talk to you on my trips to Washington." As for me, it made no difference what happened. Our friendship, the connection I felt, just was. We existed. There was no need to do anything different. I asked him how we could be friends.

He thought on this for a few moments. "We can talk about anything, yourself is fine, as long as I don't have to talk about me."

Apparently safety resided in not telling too much.

Before I left he said we could be friends and also suggested we take two steps back. The two sentiments were in direct conflict with one another, but I didn't mind.

He hugged me and kissed my cheek before I left.

As always, I was relieved that the guides had it right; they had not led me astray. All had gone well. Once more, I had done what I was asked to do. At home, I talked with the guides.

See how well this went? Write Aaron. Tell him you love him.

"You're kidding, right? Are you sure of this? What will happen if I tell him?"

But you must. You yourself feel the liberation of your talk with him. Do not be afraid to love. Do not worry. Your relationship is better than ever.

"I trust this place of being friends, but is it really okay to write such a letter? Wasn't it enough that we talked?"

You will know the truth, and the truth will set you free.

"And love is the truth."

Yes.

"How important is it to communicate further about this?"

Very. Let go of expectations about how things should go. This is what divides the past from the future. A new day. It's not clear what Aaron will do. It depends on his resolve and willingness to be open, but it will touch him. He will manage this fine. We guides can know others' intent, but we don't know their behavior in advance. How it plays out, we cannot know. We only know that it is right.

"I am so afraid that I make up these words."

All words come from a source and materialize within you. With us, you translate what we are saying. You're doing fine. No serious mistakes.

"I am aware of word choices I could make when recording your voices."

Yes, but it is all right. If you miss something or get off track, we will correct it. We are here to serve. We can only help as you let us. We are a light that you must turn on. It's as simple on your part as flipping a switch. The rest is up to us.

"This is unconditional love, spiritual love. Loving and letting go."

Precisely. Be prepared to say what you have to say, then allow things to unfold, while being very loving in all of your life. Tell the truth and let go of it. It cannot ultimately hurt him or anyone.

I wrote Aaron the letter, thanking him for the time together and for being open to my request to be friends. I told him that I had no expectations of what that would look like. I loved him and all was well.

The trip to Washington was a turning point. I had done as I was directed. I wondered how I could ever doubt myself or my inner guidance again. In a counseling session with Louise, I wrote this statement:

"I need a new belief system that allows me to know that I am important to these relationships and to the work we are accomplishing together; indeed, I am crucial to it until the work is completed. There is no way I can be left behind, even though I may not know what form my role will take until I take it."

If I really believed this, I would have to give up all vestiges of intimidation and powerlessness, as well as my limited view of myself. Yet despite my intentions, I knew I would still be nervous around Al.

Later the guides spoke: *Give it up. Find a chance to demonstrate that you are no longer afraid.*

"It is quite a role Al is playing in my life, isn't it? Dragging me like a reluctant mule into a different understanding about who I am and what I can be. No wonder I've had so many dreams about him! I do not need to explain anything to him. All I need to do is shift in my perceptions, to understand that his role is to spur my personal development, and he will know it has happened."

I called Aaron at the end of April and mentioned my recent letter. He seemed ill at ease, but the conversation went well. He told me that he had pondered my question about ridding the world of nuclear weapons and found a way to do it.

I thought the fact that he had figured this out, given his usual stance on nuclear weapons, was nothing short of miraculous. It affirmed for me why I was doing this work.

The guides commented afterwards: *It is a healing you perform if you give it freely. Others cannot help but receive it if you don't try to hang onto it in some way.*

"I fear that my role in this situation won't matter ultimately."

And you feel this in spite of the changes you see?

"Perhaps I won't do it right. I have to work hard to do the right thing or it will flop."

Nonsense. This one is in the plan. You can't screw it up. The relationships go so far back, and you have been drawn together for centuries. We believe that a culmination in the relationships and in the work you do together will happen in this life.

Pilgrimage.

I lived in a heightened state of awareness throughout this time. The dreams, the interactions on Capitol Hill, the sense of being guided every step of my journey—all brought a feeling of aliveness. I had left the familiar to embark on a pilgrimage, not knowing where the path would lead. Destiny continued to call me to tasks I wasn't sure I could carry out. But in the call, I knew somehow that I was the one for the job. Why else call *me*?

The summer that I was seven, the mother of one of my friends read. *Pilgrim's Progress* to us neighborhood children, one chapter per week. We sat on the floor of the Morrisons' living room to follow a man named Christian on his long and dangerous journey to the Celestial City. It was both an adventure story and a Christian morality tale, in which Christian passed through the Slough of Despond and the Valley of Humiliation, encountering characters such as Faithful, Worldly Wiseman, and Giant Despair. Every week brought a new challenge, a word of encouragement, a lesson about the Christian life, or a temptation to fall by the wayside. Thus I was introduced to the pilgrim's life at an early age.

The sequence of four lives I supposedly shared with Gore represented a pilgrimage through time, from ancient Egypt to the plains of northern U.S. to Washington, D.C. Although I had no confirmation that the stories were true, they served to explain the need I felt to help him now. If this were India, Native America, West Africa, or aboriginal Australia—if I lived in a Hindu or Buddhist culture—no one would question the validity of the information about past lives. The one who had received such insights would be revered and granted deep respect.

The Old Testament includes numerous examples of prophets returning to the world for a second or third time. Among the Jews who waited for the Messiah, many believed that Jesus was the reincarnation of the prophet Elijah. Indeed, the early Christian Church taught reincarnation for almost five hundred years. It is a fact that Jesus himself did not counter this belief.

In the end, it mattered little to me if the stories were true. My sense of connection to these men, to the work I was doing, and to my own destiny was undeniable. I had only to listen to the nudgings of Spirit and my own soul and to keep following the path.

8
Psychic Analysis

It was a tumultuous time for me, and my friends could see it. Everyone tried to be helpful; it's what friends are for. Within the space of a week, two of them told me about Phyliss Moline, another psychic who had recently settled in the Nashville area. I wasn't sure I wanted to visit another psychic. When my massage therapist, the third friend to recommend Phyliss, said, "Go see Phyliss Moline. She can help with your neck and shoulders," I called to make an appointment.

May 2, 1985. Phyliss greeted me at the door and introduced me to her assistant, a white-haired man named Duke who towered above her. Phyliss was in her late thirties with waves of sandy brown hair, sparkling brown eyes, and a feeling of softness about her. We went into a small bare room at the back of her office, just three chairs and a wood table. As we seated ourselves for the session, Phyliss turned to Duke. "This is going to be big. I can feel it. We need to record this one." Duke pulled a tape recorder out of a satchel and wrote the date on a blank tape.

Phyliss closed her eyes and prayed: "Use us as a healing light to all brought here by name or thought."

Duke turned on the recorder, and Phyliss shifted in her seat to face me squarely. "You are making very quick movement spiritually. Movement on the physical plane is not as fast. The result is that there is a sensation of loss; in fact, there is no loss. You are clearing your emotions." She smiled good-naturedly. "Are you moving into a relationship now?"

I thought she meant Aaron and nodded yes.

"Do not be in relationship right now." Phyliss said this with equanimity, no hint of blame. "It's time to be within the self. Be receptive and keep centered. No other action. Anything that would pull *you* away from *you* is not advisable. You are in a spiritual transit from January until September."

I noted the dates: January 1st was the day I came home from Kripalu, resolved to heal the pain in my neck.

"You must clear judgment and fear out of you. Your cycle of spirituality is just beginning. Before, there was a denial of your spiritual connection and your intuition. That denial is going away."

This felt right to me. My dreams, the voices, even the lightning bolt, had been urging me to step out of denial and acknowledge my spirituality and my intuition.

"This time of spiritual movement is helping you clear old pain and fear. It is a time of cleansing, which ungrounds us. In the fall, relationships can be done with less pain and more choice." Phyliss paused. "Do you have any dark visions?"

"No."

"Do you have any voices?"

"Yes, I do." This surprised me. How could she know to ask that? How many people have voices?

"Do they talk to you about pain and sorrow?"

"No, the voices are very positive."

I told the story of the lightning bolt, the pain in my neck and shoulders, my role in halting the arms race, and the issue of trusting my own judgment. I told her I had come to see her because of the physical pain. Then I described the screen in my head with the *yes/no* answers, how I had asked the screen if I was doing the right things to heal my neck, how the voices spoke to me. I was trying to follow what the voices told me to do. I asked them a lot of questions.

When I finished talking, I realized that, of course, the voices had been talking to me about pain!

"The voices just want you to be healed. They don't care about anything else." A sweet smile, kindness in her voice. "All that healing, don't apply action to it. Anything dealing with pain, they'll say yes to. Be real careful how you phrase the questions. Let the relationship pass through the pain level, then you can go into the relationship with clarity and understanding. Ask: 'What is the pain in my neck directed to?' But do not put action to it.

"Your guides are going to remove the pain, by love and by energy. Yours are good guides." She nodded to affirm this statement. "They work to shift your consciousness. Energy and love have no action to it. If they say yes to clearing the relationship, they mean heal the relationship, don't act. Sitting and healing.

"Expression should be completely verbal. Be friends. You can write, talk on the phone, etc., but not be out of yourself. Be in spiritual harmony with this person. You don't have to mix it up with the rest of your life."

"Okay. Yes, I see."

"The psyche is opening all up—that's good. Not all psychic energy is positive or good. Your guides are good, but the information can get cluttered from other psyches out in the atmosphere and you telepathically pick them up. Move into feeling 'essence.' Be in the essence, relating to the Universe in all its spiritual essence, not just in its physical or emotional spheres."

I heard her words, but I didn't fully understand what this meant.

"First, the voices, then some type of Buddha or Christ consciousness. That way no judgment is applied to what the voices tell you. Right now there's too much judgment on the information."

She continued. "Yours are very joyous, clean guides. Two females, three males."

I was astonished. The voices had told me there were five!

"You have opened up to psychic energy in order to hear the voices. Next is a spiritual step. The psyche has limitation; spiritual healing has no limitation. Your shoulders will hurt as the psyche develops. Victim consciousness, subservience, and will—all are moving out. Your shoulders are holding the brain down. It's hard work!"

I knew all too well about victim consciousness and will! I'd had to relinquish my will over and over in order to do what Spirit was asking of me.

This session with Phyliss was unlike anything I had experienced before. She was a locomotive roaring through my consciousness, shining a light on everything in its path.

"When the voices say 'tell them I love them' (good guides do this), hold the person's name inside your heart and say, 'I forgive myself for being in this time and space.' Lose judgment and have forgiveness for all of them and for yourself. You are moving eventually into more service. It will be clear in September and you won't need to worry about the actions you take.

"Other people around you have voices, too, don't they?"

I nodded. One friend started channeling an "entity" about the same time that my voices appeared, independent of me. Another, intrigued when my voices showed up, asked for voices to speak to her two weeks later.

"Others' voices are a diversion for you. Theirs are not like yours. Yours are different. Try to ask your voices something besides what's happening with pain. For example, 'I'm happy. Why?'"

I told her a recent dream in which I was in an elevator and pushed the button to go to Level 9. When I got out, there was a meeting with the mayor of Nashville. A woman named Sandra Prouen D'oun was seated next to the mayor. (When I woke up I knew it was Sandra Day O'Connor, the Supreme Court Justice.) She was there to tell me how to get to the next level—the spiritual level. In the meeting, the mayor felt ashamed about something. At the end of the dream, he was relieved. He got up and shook my hand.

"The dream is about your shame, old shame," said Phyliss. "Nine is a completion, out of the pain, and Sandra represents justice being made. The mayor has something to be ashamed about, too, and he is healed in the dream. Thank you for healing the mayor." She smiled as she told me this.

The tape ran out, and Duke did not have another. I began taking notes on a legal pad I had brought with me.

The dreams about Gore weighed on my mind. I was hesitant to ask, not wanting to reveal anything about the relationship, but I felt I needed to know what Phyliss had to say about them, so I plunged in.

"I've had forty-plus dreams about a man I work with. Can you tell me what these are about?"

"I know who this is," she said. "We have a group that prays for him every Sunday night." Then she named him: Al Gore, Jr.

I stared at her in disbelief.

"His role has death in it. You know this is about death, don't you?" She said this as a matter of fact, but the words shook me.

I leaned forward. Perhaps I hadn't heard her correctly. "You mean the deaths of our sisters? His sister and my sister died under very similar circumstances. He and I were both thirty-six years old when our sisters, our only siblings, died of cancer."

"No, not your sisters. The dreams are about *his* death, a heart attack. A mini heart attack."

"*His* death?" Oh, my God! Tears came to my eyes. "How can that be?"

"He is ruled by his mental body. He is in deep emotional pain from taking on the pain of the world. Ask your guides to send him love. He is a catalyst whose energies are crucial to what is happening in the world. The arms control scene and change is happening by virtue of his presence, not his mental activity or strategy.

"Your dreams have been trying to tell you he is in danger. He needs someone to talk to and has no one. You must go to him and warn him about his health. No one else can do it. Only you."

I shook my head, not wanting to believe what she was saying. I was frightened for Al, and my tears were about this.

But I was also frightened for me. As if the voices, the dreams, and the lightning bolt had not asked enough of me, I was supposed to do this, too? Phyliss and Duke watched me and said nothing.

My mind scanned the dreams. I couldn't remember anything about his death and told her so.

"The messages are there," she said quietly. "This talking to Gore is an exception to what I've told you about waiting until September. Do it."

I could not imagine going to Al to tell him that his life was in danger and that my dreams had issued the warning.

I handed Phyliss my astrological chart, which I had brought with me. She studied it for a few moments. "Your chart says that this lifetime is about making friends with your enemies. It is a time for making forgiveness and being friends with those who have been your enemies in the past, and for forgiving yourself for past wrongdoings."

"The voices told me about past lives with Al and Aaron."

"Good! They were probably right. Did they tell you about the pioneer life? Or the occult one?"

How on earth could she know this? These were the two lives where we were enemies! Phyliss' knowing stunned me. "The voices described a prairie life where Al saved my life after he and other soldiers killed my family, and a life in ancient Egypt, where I knew both Al and Aaron. I was a judge and issued a decree that had Al killed."

"I see." She nodded at Duke, whose eyes had grown quite large, then looked back at me. "You will move to be a healer, past the psychic level."

Phyliss signaled Duke with a dip of her head. The session was over.

———————————

The Oracle.

How does the subconscious make itself aware in consciousness? And where does one go for verification that its messages are true? Despite my concern about the task that lay before me, and although it might be weeks before I knew the truth of Phyliss' warning, I felt the wisdom of her words for me. In my experience, Phyliss was an oracle.

Oracles have existed in cultures as diverse as China, India, Tibet, Sub-Saharan Africa, and Pre-Columbian America. As well, Celts, Hindus, Christians, Buddhists, Greeks, Jews, and others have called on oracles to offer wise counsel or knowledge of the future, believing they were inspired by the gods. The oracle was thought to be the portal through which God spoke directly to the people. It is true that some claiming to be psychic are not the purest channels of divine wisdom. One needs to use common sense and one's own heart to judge if the truth is being spoken, whether by a psychic, astrologer, psychologist, or priest.

The dreams and voices that came to me were from another realm—sometimes eerily precise, often mysterious. This stream of messages seemed intent on guiding my actions. Many in America would think me crazy for consulting an oracle. In other countries, other cultures, other times, one would be considered crazy not to.

In much of the world, intuitives, mystics, seers, shamans, priests, rabbis, and others in touch with the realms of Spirit are viewed as the mouthpiece of divine inspiration. These people often sit next to the king or queen to offer sage advice. Abraham and Mary Lincoln consulted a medium who held séances at the White House; other leaders in high offices have consulted astrologers, mystics, and seers. Everyone in a high position seeks counsel, and well that they should.

9
The Heart Is a Shrine

May 2, 1985. On the drive home following the session, blood pounded in my temples and my head ached. I felt overwhelmed by the possibility that Al's life was in danger and that it was my task to tell him. How on earth would I do this? What would I say was the source of my information?

Louise, our friend Mauni Mitchel, and I had planned to co-counsel at my house that afternoon, and I was running late. When I arrived, they were sitting in my living room waiting for me.

Louise gave me a hug. "How was your visit with the psychic?"

"Unbelievable." I tossed the tape of my session with Phyliss onto an end table.

They exchanged glances.

"*Good* unbelievable?" asked Mauni.

"I don't know. I'm stunned. That's all I can say."

They knew they would hear about it in my counseling session. As we pulled our chairs together for the session, Louise said, "Oh, by the way, Al Gore will be in town tomorrow, speaking at Tennessee State University. I'm going. Would you like to go?"

I shook my head in utter disbelief. "Wait till you hear what I am supposed to do."

Al Gore spoke publicly in Nashville about once a month. Many of his speeches were fundraisers or events by invitation only. The university speech was the first open event I'd heard of in quite a while.

That night I dreamed about backing out of a garage, trying to park the car and backing over a ledge. Clearly, some part of me wanted to back out.

I decided to take six-year-old Amy with me, who asked to wear her hair in a *beebee*, a Korean word for a little ponytail worn on top of the head. In the pink-flowered dress she chose for the occasion, she looked like a fairy princess. We met Louise outside the building and took seats in the smallish auditorium, Amy sitting on my lap.

Gore's speech was animated, full of personal references, as he knew many people in the audience. He talked about his priorities if he were elected senator and described potential cooperation between Nashville's African-American and Caucasian communities. I could hardly focus on his words, convinced that when I told him afterwards why I wanted to meet with him, he would refuse the one-on-one meeting and decide to stop talking to me altogether.

Gore received a standing ovation, then everyone filed out the door, anticipating a chance to shake his hand. This man, their friend, was about to become a U.S. senator. I waited until everyone else had passed through the line. Finally, I stepped forward, clasping Amy by the hand.

He looked down at Amy, tilted his head, and smiled. "Very cute," he said. Amy ducked behind me, shy but smiling back. For a few moments, there was a little game between them, with Amy peeking out from behind my skirt.

Then the game was over, and Al looked at me quizzically, waiting for me to speak.

I congratulated him on the speech, then took a deep breath. The time had come; I mustered my courage. "I'd like an appointment to talk with you privately."

He nodded. "What is the topic?"

"Your health," I ventured. My stomach ached from the tension.

"My health?" He laughed. "And where did you get this information?"

"I've told you before that I've had many dreams about our working together. Well, I sought help with understanding the dreams."

"A shaman, perhaps?" His eyes twinkled and he was grinning at me.

"Yes, perhaps."

His expression turned serious. "Call Peter and ask him to make an appointment the next time I'm in town."

"Okay. Thank you. I will."

Later that day I talked to the voices: "I am confused over whether to trust you. Why didn't you tell me about the meaning of the dreams? Is Phyliss right about Al's danger?"

"Yes, absolutely. We wanted you to hear it from someone besides us first. It's too easy to doubt yourself. Phyliss confirmed many things for you, so that by the time she told you about your dreams, you trusted her. It's the only way you could receive this information and know it was true.

"What is the fear about, regarding Al? It seems so much heavier than the current circumstances would warrant. Why do I feel terrified of telling him about the messages of the dreams?"

The fear comes from opening yourself to loving unconditionally. The love opens the door on all the remaining fear. You fear that you will impose on him or that you will get lost in your feelings. There is also fear from past lives. What a paradox! You have each been responsible for the other's death, and he has saved your life. Now you have information that will save his life. You hold a key to his life. Everyone holds keys to many lives, by the way—by avoiding hitting someone with your car, helping a person through depression, and so on.

"Why have the dreams not been more explicit about the danger?"

Go back and read them. You will find many signs.

May 6. I went back through the dreams. Several showed Gore aging fast, graying, with thinning hair. In one, he wore a tattered black coat, too short for him, exposing skinny legs. He was not well. In another, he was poor, downcast, and weak. In yet another dream Al was older and balding. The following night, I dreamed he arrived in an old car.

Then there was the dream about the death of someone. The first and last parts of the dream were about Al speaking to a group. In the middle "there was a death somewhere" and warnings of three boy children dying, carried by their fathers. I had written in the margin: "A dream of missed opportunities for me." Something in me knew I had missed important clues.

May 9. I called Peter and requested the appointment with Gore on his next visit to Nashville. There wasn't time to talk at length, but Peter agreed to look at Al's schedule. I could tell he was uncertain about why I was asking for this. Afterwards I wondered whether to call Peter back and tell him what this was about.

I went into meditation to quiet my thoughts, then asked, "Should I call Peter again?"

Tell him. It's not easy, we know. Peter will understand enough to let you through to Al.

"It feels difficult, telling Peter. He doesn't known about the previous dreams. He's had no preparation for this."

You know what to say. This is not a secret. It is not occult. Nor is it a hasty decision. You've put off talking to Peter for a long time. It will increase rather than decrease his respect for you, of which there is already a great deal. It will set him on his heels—do not fear this change. Peter can handle it. He needs to know what you are about. He is your ally. As for Al, telling him about the dreams is perfect. We predict a sea change for Al, a healing. Much good will come of it.

"I have many dreams of being in a cafeteria, where I go through the line, sit down, and eat. In some of these dreams, Al is watching me."

Al is not nourishing himself well. In the dreams Al watches you choose foods that are good for you, in order to learn from you. Al needs to observe his own feelings and intuition, what is deep in his heart. These dreams are an important aspect of the message that is intended for Al.

May 12. I was still afraid of talking to Peter, which I kept putting off. My neck hurt, which was throbbing from the fear. "Dear voices, do you have advice to help me become calmer and work through this fear?"

We are here. It is harder to come through when you are so tense. Relax. Close your eyes and meditate for a moment. We will speak to you.

After a few moments of meditation I asked, "Will I leave this fear behind one day?"

Yes. A wonderful July is coming for you. You can let the fear go. It will pass through you in your counseling sessions, and it will also go as you learn to trust this reality which feels new to you.

I meditated again, for a longer time. When I opened my eyes, the voices returned.

You see how easily you tap into the calmness within? The fear is on its way out. Have faith that this is truth. Al will survive your fear. You can go to him with complete self-assurance. Practice this: "I am calmly assured. I know what I know. What I bring to them is a gift beyond measure." Read. Meditate. Feel your own inner strength.

I still felt intensely frustrated. Finally, in desperation, I said to the guides, "Okay, I'm ready. Use me however you like!"

———————

May 13. "Can you help me take a different viewpoint on what is happening? To see it as the gift that it is?"

You understand this as a gift for Al, which it is. It is also a gift for you. Al doesn't know the level at which you are struggling to be free. Your responsibility here is not primarily to Al, but to yourself. We have given you a task that you cannot not do, and thereby we hope to hasten your movement. We know that the roots of your caring about Al go back in time, seemingly forever. How could you possibly turn away now, when the moment has come to make amends for something you did 3,000 years ago? We know you cannot. It is by correcting this past wrong that you will come to know your true self.

I shared this writing with Linda, who said, "The energy of metamorphosis is like a speeding freight train. It can't be stopped. You're struggling both not to die and not to be reborn. By struggling you only make the passage more difficult. You've invited this change. It's not happening against your will. It's a radical change, a change of essence and consciousness."

May 14. When I awoke, I remembered two dreams:

Dream #1: *The white train comes every half hour at the end of the day to take us home. We work not far from where it stops. One has to gather all one's white clothes and get to the train in time in order to get home. Mauni gathers up her son's white clothes. I go to the station and make it neat, lining up flowers and papers so there will be room for the train.*

Dream #2: *I am outdoors with a group of people. A man says he wants to go to a nearby shrine that is dedicated to the Germans. I want to go, too, so we go together. On the way, there is an aerobics class. I am interested in the class, but decide to continue to the shrine, which is like a church. When we arrive, I take the man's hand, which surprises him. I see it as a way to offer healing. There is a four-foot missile buried under concrete, pointing toward East Germany; also a white refrigerator full of white food (milk and almonds), and a box of matches.*

The dreams were full of spiritual symbolism: a white train

(pure light and energy) that was taking me home to myself, to the real me who acted without fear; an aerobics class for healing the physical heart; and a shrine for healing the spiritual and emotional heart. The shrine dedicated to the divided Germany offered the hope of healing the heart of its divisions.

The man in the dream was Al. We were going to the heart of things: his heart needing to be healed, the two warring sides (East and West), and the threat of nuclear war. The dream was about healing through honoring the pain and divisiveness of Germany. It was also about nourishing ourselves spiritually.

I shared this dream with Louise in a co-counseling session, who said, "Caroline, the physical touch is exactly right. It is healing and will heal almost regardless of what you say or what else happens."

I named the dreams, "I Prepare to Heal the Heart."

May 20. I still had not spoken to Peter. I had been working hard and felt very tired. I knew that once I spoke with Peter, there was no turning back. I would have to tell Al. I wondered how I could let go of the tension and fear. The voices responded:

Stay tuned in to us, the light inside. Think love. As the fear subsides, the love will be there. It hasn't gone anywhere. Call Peter again. You need to clear that one up. Talk to him about the dreams and the warning about Al's health. Phone him today.

I knew I had to do this. I sat for a few minutes in silence, calling the feeling of love into my heart. I knew that if I was "in love," I would not be "in fear" when I called Peter. *Yes*, I thought, *I am willing to be led from the innermost place.*

I took a deep breath and dialed the phone. When Peter came on the line, I told him I'd had many dreams about Al, and that the dreams seemed to be a warning about his health. I told him this was why I had asked for the meeting with Al.

"Wow." Peter paused briefly. "Caroline, it's obvious a higher consciousness is speaking through you. What a powerful relationship compared to other relationships! I can see how you would feel driven to take care of this."

My relief was enormous. I got off the phone and breathed in the relief. How incredible that Peter would understand! Then I heard the voices:

Peter has seen and heard the truth of who you are. When you meet with Al, remember that you are there to offer healing. Your presence alone will heal. Your words will be heard. He will act on it, and he will be grateful.

I remembered something I wanted to ask the voices. "Lately, when I close my eyes, I see the color red."

Red is the color of blood. Blood of the lamb. Blood of sacrifice. This task feels and is a sacrifice, in the truest, purest sense. As though shedding your blood to save Al's life. Giving of your very soul.

Red is the color of the heart.

Take Heart.

When I was a young woman, I saw the movie, "The Heart Is a Lonely Hunter," based on Carson McCullers' novel by the same name. I was deeply affected by the story of a teenager seeking her soul and her identity through music, and the deaf mute who committed suicide out of loneliness. The story echoed the profound loneliness I felt as an adolescent and young adult.

The heart is indeed alone in its search for connection and meaning, although the world opens before us, offering light and direction if we but notice. I hoped to be a light for Al Gore in a manner that was outside what others thought was rational. Voices and dreams, indeed.

My mission was heartfelt. I believed I had his interests at heart.

Together we would go to the heart of the matter.

Would he take it to heart?

Would he take heart? Or lose heart?

Heartbeat. Heart-to-heart.

Heart attack.

A change of heart.

Yes, yes, open the heart.

10
The Meeting

Peter called to say that I would meet with Gore on May 29 after a major fundraising speech at the Opryland Hotel, outside of Nashville. Before going to sleep, I asked for a dream of healing and acceptance of the truth and rightness of what I had been doing and was about to do. I prayed for Al's preparation to receive the messages. During the night there were intense thunder storms and the electricity went out.

In the seven days that preceded our meeting, my dreams had more images of "back" and "backing up." Sitting in the back seat, going out the back door. Once again, some part of me desperately wanted to back out. On the night before the meeting, I dreamed about the meeting itself:

May 28. *Al arrives at the hotel for our meeting, and I excuse myself to go to the bathroom, where I freshen up to prepare for a ceremony. Meanwhile, Al falls asleep, and I decide to let him sleep, thinking he needs rest, even though time has almost run out. Peter arrives. "It is urgent now," I tell him. "It must be done as soon as possible." Alarmed, Peter says, "Okay." We try to wake Al. I put my hand on his "back." Al is disoriented, and it is difficult to wake him up.*

By now, I had remembered and written down forty-nine dreams about Al. A "prodigious" number of dreams in every sense of that word ... an enormous amount ... portentous, as an omen ... strange and unusual ... amazing and wondrous.

Was this final dream a premonition about how he would take the warning regarding his health? Would it be difficult for Al to wake up? I asked the voices.

He is in some sense no different from any human being who is not yet awake. Your information about his impending death is the best you can give him right now. It will facilitate growth in him, which is what we are after.

As I prepared myself emotionally for the meeting, I also stewed over how to work with him—what to say and do—given his latest political maneuver. "What about this Star Wars compromise that he facilitated? The billions of dollars it would take to create a shield that would protect the U.S. from incoming Soviet missiles? Why not negotiate for both sides to stop building and dismantle weapons instead?"

Completely misguided. You are right. We wonder at the persistence of this pattern in him.

"What can I say to Al about this, and to Aaron?"

Say: It grieves me to see you making this mistake again.

"How can I meet with him when I am so angry about the compromise?"

You can and will do it. It's a test of your ability to forgive. Can you forgive someone who kills and destroys? The killing and destroying aspect of him is a carryover from the past. He is learning more about his power to kill or to save. He wants to save—you can see this. Few people understand that the means are never a justification for the end.

"Is this true?"

Absolutely. It is a karmic law.

"What about war? Killing the enemy in order to save one's country?"

It is never justified.

"Self-defense?"

It's the only exception, and only as a last resort. Being committed to an approach that focuses on building more nuclear weapons leaves out the victims—the citizens held hostage by the arms race.

All I knew was that the meeting to talk about Al's health was not the place to discuss Star Wars. It would wait for another day.

May 29. I arrived at the Opryland Hotel at 10:30 p.m. just as Al was finishing his speech. Al's staff had been instructed to let me in at the door. The ballroom was packed for this $1000-a-plate dinner, and the mood was gay. The audience was very appreciative of Al's speech; loud applause followed each of his key points.

My eyes were on the man at the podium. I trembled as I waited for the speech to conclude and the ensuing throng to disperse. I had not slept well for three weeks, the adrenaline coursing through me like an icy stream.

One of Gore's staff took me to a nearby room to wait. I glanced around. I had never seen a room quite like this. Not a large room, and not well lit. Was it a reception room? There were tweedy sofas, end tables, and lamps. I chose the end of a sofa that faced the door and focused on my breath, willing myself to relax, although my heart was racing. Racing to get somewhere, but where? How far could this conversation go?

Al arrived and greeted me with a brief hug. He sat down across from me, next to a table and lamp, then crossed his legs and straightened his jacket. Both of us were enveloped in dim yellow light.

We exchanged pleasantries, but I was shaking.

"Good speech," I said, "and a welcoming audience."

"How's your family?"

"The children are well."

"And Ron?"

"He is well, too. And your family?"

"Everyone is fine."

We paused. This was my cue. This was one of the toughest gaps of silence I had ever had to bridge.

"As you know, I want to talk to you about your health." There, I'd said it.

He nodded.

"I've had many dreams about you now, close to fifty. It is unbelievable to me but it's true. I've gone to someone for help in understanding what they are about. The woman I met with

111

told me that many are about your health. She said they are a warning, and that it is essential that I share this with you."

"What exactly do the dreams say?"

"That you are aging prematurely. That you need to take better care of yourself. This woman says that you are in danger of a heart attack. She says that you need someone to talk to, that you have no one, and that this task falls to me. I felt I had to pass this message on to you."

"I don't know about your source of information." He was clearly skeptical, but why shouldn't he be? "It's hard for me to see that a woman who doesn't know me could have accurate information about my life. But thank you." Al seemed stiff, humorless, and tense.

"I can imagine you would feel that way." I waited for his next response.

He stared at me hard, then shifted in his seat. "What do you do to take care of *your*self?"

"I meditate and do yoga. I try to walk every day. I also use a process called co-counseling, where another person and I take turns listening to each other talk about what troubles us. Do you have anyone to listen to you?"

"Everyone around me is invested in what happens to me. I pray, but I have no counselor."

Years later, when I convened workshops on lobbying from the heart, inviting members of Congress and activists to discuss ways we could support our elected officials, these members conveyed the same message to us. They had no one to talk to; everyone was invested in the outcome.

Neither Al nor I spoke for a few moments, and I wondered what he was thinking. There were long pauses throughout this conversation. I looked at him quizzically at one point, waiting for him to speak. He shrugged ever so slightly. "I edit everything before I speak. Sad, but true."

He excused himself and went to the bathroom that was connected to this room. I hadn't noticed a bathroom, but I remembered my dream of the previous night, of me going to an adjoining bathroom to freshen up for a ceremony. And so it was Al who prepared for a ceremony—a spiritual initiation, perhaps.

Al returned in a few minutes with a strange expression on his face. I could not read what he was thinking.

"Thank you for being so courageous," he said. "I'm sure it wasn't easy to do."

He remained standing, so I stood up. He embraced me, but he seemed to be somewhere else, not quite present, almost cold, as though the real Al Gore was not at home.

I took a step back and placed my hands over his heart for just a moment, then dropped them to my side. "I pray that what I have said will be of help in some way."

There was no softness in his voice when he said, "I want no involvement. I have worried about your dreams, afraid they were not good for you. I felt perhaps I should withdraw from you."

"No, please, I would hate to lose you as a friend. I have been confused at times about what all this means, but even in that confusion, I have not looked for a romantic or physical relationship. I still don't."

He seemed satisfied with my answer. "Okay, I'll take this as a warning, and I'll call or write you to let you know how it goes."

I had done what I had to do.

Book Two: Unwrapping the Gift

Book of the Dead.

I'd had forty-nine dreams about Al Gore, Jr., over the course of two years. Dreams of communicating with him at what seemed to be another level of existence. Dreams of my own empowerment, our work together, his health and well-being, and warnings about his death.

In *The Tibetan Book of the Dead*, there are forty-nine days of transition after one dies. During those forty-nine days, the teacher who knows about death communicates with the soul that is in a perilous transition, unsure of where it is to go. The soul has the opportunity for complete absolution and making it to the highest heights, or for being thrown back into the land of pain, suffering, birth, and death.

The past life stories I had been told about Al and myself said that this life was the fourth in a series—a completion—and that I was here to save his life, similar to the lama or *rinpoche* with the task of guiding the lost soul through the realms of pain and suffering. What qualifies the lama is having successfully navigated the realms for him or herself.

I wonder, always, about my role in relation to Al, why I was called to this task. The best I can understand, even now, is that by successfully navigating the messages of the voices, stories of past lives, and dreams from another world, I had completed an initiation that prepared me to meet him at the Opryland Hotel that fateful night.

In myths, the spiritual adept goes to the depths of the underworld and brings back a gift. I, too, had placed a gift at Al's feet and left it for him to collect.

11
Where Triumph Lies

I returned home breathless, exhilarated and relieved that I had completed my task. The significance of what I had done did not elude me. Al returned to Washington. I suspected that weeks might pass before I heard from him.

Grateful that Al had said he would act on the warning despite his distrust of my sources of information, I also left our encounter keenly aware of his aloneness and vulnerability and in touch with my own.

When I spoke to the voices about the meeting, they said, *Treasure the friendship. Remember his pain. Tread lightly.*

On the second night, Al visited me in a dream. He was cheerful and light-hearted; his face bright and untroubled. It was a dream-world assurance that all was well.

I spoke to the guides: "I sense that the dreams that come after our recent encounter are not to be shared with Al. Rather, they are mine alone. Is this true?"

Yes, it is true. Future dream messages are for "your eyes only." Al does need to hear from you. You intuit this. Offer the assurance that all is well between you.

"What would your words be to him?"

"Our words" in "your words"? Ha-ha!

"Yes."

Dear Al. I love you. I've been wanting for some time to tell you what I mean by this: This love is a state of existence, unconditional, without regard to any behavior or response on your part. It just is. It's a matter of fact. I accept and value our recent meeting on those terms. No corruption of the relationship. No discouragement.

"I cannot believe that I should tell him this. What will he think of this?"

Offer to be his friend. Remember that it is a gift. Can you imagine anyone in your life giving you such a gift?

Time passed slowly. I prayed and meditated often, but I did not contact Al as the voices suggested. The letter they proposed was beyond what I was able to say to him. I focused on my family, my mother, and my writing. Much went well.

On June 5, 1985, remembering Phyliss' advice, I asked the voices, "Why do I feel happy?"

Happiness is contentment is blessing. God's in her heaven inside you; all's right with the world. You are our messenger, our flag in the world. Remember that you are of God. God's essence is you. You need never fear or worry about another thing. Imagine! A life without fear. Lay down your life and your fear. Follow the voice of Spirit in the world. We will not mislead you or direct you astray. Pray and meditate as often as you can.

"What would my life be like without fear?"

Lovely. Beautiful. Radiant. The light in your eyes and on your face will transform them. They will be visibly moved by your light. You have done splendid thinking about how to bring about peace. You have taken risks and built relationships without compromising your ideals and goals. Remember: If Al in his role is able to accept the dream messages, then there is hope for everyone.

"If I could really trust these messages and always live from this place of peace, what a profound effect it would have on my life!"

June 6. "Will the book I'm writing about Cathy ever be published?"

Relax. You are fine. The book may or may not happen. Don't push it. Take things as they come. You keep trying to create the future. You can't! Put your attention on feeling love within you and loving those around you. Al will call, and you will talk to him, and you will be happy with the result. What you offer is healing, wholeness, health. He knows this. Your words, whether by phone or on paper, will help him. Love heals. Remember this with everyone.

"And my neck, which continues to bother me?"

Is in divine order. It's coming along just fine. Keep talking to us, meditating, co-counseling with Louise. All is in divine order. You're doing great. Believe us, because we know!

On June 20, I returned to see Phyliss. As we chatted, she told me that my relationship with Al was "smooth and thick, like a cabinet top. It's a very large, expanding relationship. He's not clear now but will be ready to talk to you soon." She added, "I can tell that you are clear about the relationship. You can go ahead and write to him this week or next. It's ready for action. Tell him what you're feeling and where you're feeling clear."

Al called within the week. His voice was light and happy. He sounded relaxed. He was exercising several days a week at the congressional gym, eating healthier food, and working shorter hours. His weight had dropped; his blood pressure had dropped. He felt more at ease and was sleeping better, too. Al thanked me for my help. He thanked me for having the courage to speak to him.

All was well, indeed.

That evening I penned the letter to Gore, similar to what the guides had suggested. I considered the boldness of this letter and asked the voices if I needed to change it in any way.

No, it is fine.

"I am very busy with my family and work, I tell the voices. If it's not right, I don't have time to change it."

There's always time to do it right. That's what time is!
Such wisdom. I laughed.

It seemed that a radical change was in the wind, but I didn't know yet what that change was. Before going to sleep, I asked myself about the meaning of my life. I seldom felt deeply happy and didn't know why this was true, although I suspected its roots were in childhood. I wondered if happiness was a rational goal. If so, how could I get there? Was the answer inside me? That night I dreamed:

Al is talking to a small group of people that includes me. I ask him a question, then answer it myself: "It's about people getting close, then separating, then getting close, then separating. A cycle of connecting with others and learning how to be with one's self." After the meeting I say to him, "I believe I've discovered what life is all about."

I called Phyliss. "Gore is out of danger," she said. "Thank you."

I told her that I had been having prescient dreams about car accidents and events that involved people I knew. Insights into people's lives had come in the form of messages about what was happening to them and what they needed to do about it. Sometimes I had flashes of insight about my own and others' past lives.

"You are an absent healer with energy flowing through you to other people several times a day," Phyliss said. "The pain at the back of your neck is an indication you have just healed someone. You are clairsentient, able to tune into people's emotions and heal them."

The term was new to me. She said that clairsentience involved healing the emotional energy of a number of people at once. "It will wear you out if you're unaware that it's happening. I must teach you how to take care of yourself." Phyliss added that there were only two hundred of us in the U.S., including herself and me. She offered to teach me to be a healer.

I knew that I was already a healer, that energy flowed through me to others. Phyliss' offer to teach me how to take care of myself and how to be more effective as a healer was a wonderful gift.

My thoughts drifted to Aaron Wolfe, and I wondered if it was time to reconnect with him. The guides had told me that he was on Earth at this time with a specific task: to figure out what went wrong in humanity's history. This message was very important to me. It explained, in part, why I felt drawn to him. I, too, longed to know the answer to this question.

I lacked the words to describe what I experienced in relationship to Aaron; when I thought about him, my energy increased. I had not had this experience before, but when I told Phyliss, she said she knew exactly what I was speaking of. "Not everyone would understand," she said, "but I do. It's a very good interaction of energies. You will experience this at other times in your life as well, with other people. You can learn from the situation with Aaron."

Later I asked the voices to explain this dynamic further.

It is like a particle beam between you. A very real physiological event. Each person has their own beam, of course, but the frequencies of yours and Aaron's are quite close. It's very neat, don't you think?

"Yes, I think so. And what do I do with this?"

Meditate and build on it. Use it in the rest of your life. Turn the love outward.

Two weeks later, on vacation with my family in western Massachusetts, I spoke with the guides about my friendship with Aaron.

It is important that you do not judge what Aaron represents. Allow the energy exchange to be. It need not be anything it's not. Enjoy it for what it is. Be a friend, nothing more or less. Treat him as you would yourself—your best self, warm, funny, kind.

"You've given me plenty of assurance that all is well with Aaron, but I can't seem to get clear about what to say and when."

We love you, and you love us. We are in this together. You are becoming very powerful. Your energy is expanding; indeed, it has already expanded greatly, and you feel it. It's perfect. You are gaining the ability to heal others as you tap into and allow your energy to expand and flow. God is with you. Aaron is well, too. He does love you. How could he not? Anytime a door opens to another person, love is present. Operate on this assumption.

"Really?"

Guidelines for your behavior: (1) Operate totally and completely out of your love for yourself. (2) Stay in touch with him. It will ground the relationship. (3) You must speak the truth. He will be awed by the power you represent. Truth is the ultimate power. (4) Find ways to reassure him. You have no need for him to be anything in particular. (5) Be sensitive to his difficulty, but don't back away.

August 20. "Where am I on my life's path? What do I need to know that will help me along the way?"

Remember to think "grace" and drop the expectations. In this way, the most joyful, unexpected things can happen. Expect nothing. This is wonderful training ground for you. So much to learn.

One morning I read an interview with author Richard Bach, who talked about the danger inherent in someone saying I love you. "Watch out," he said. "It's a trap. What can the woman want?" Bach was describing a cultural view of love, one that is based on desire and want.

We have just one word—*love*—to describe a range of emotional and spiritual states, wants, desire, and expectations. What Spirit was describing to me was not romantic love or love based on need and gratification. Rather, it was a state of being in which love, kindness, and compassion are flowed to others without expectation of anything in return.

I was not the only one to say "I love you" during this time. Three men in the public eye—a candidate for president, a well-known musician, and a national disarmament leader—told me they loved me within minutes of meeting me. I understood that they meant what I meant: heartfelt love and respect.

In July and August, with Phyliss' help, I became aware of the energy that flowed through my hands. The voices constantly affirmed that my role with Gore and Wolfe was to offer spiritual, emotional, and physical healing. Phyliss and the guides continued to work with me to heal the vestiges of feelings of powerlessness.

During this time I felt a strong connection to the chiropractor who was helping me heal my neck. One day while writing in a small carrel on the second floor of the Scarritt Library, a couple of miles from my house, the voices suggested a past life connection with the chiropractor—that he and I had been Pierre and Marie Curie—and how this possibility related to our present lives. This seemed preposterous to me, too glamorous. I wondered how many people believed they had been Marie Curie! I asked the voices for clarification. They offered information about her life that they said I could confirm in historical material about Madame Curie.

I traipsed downstairs to the card catalog and looked up the Curies. Indeed, the information the voices had given me was correct.

I knew that Marie Curie was brilliant, dedicated, and extraordinarily competent. She had received Nobel Peace Prizes in Chemistry and Physics for her work. During Marie Curie's lifetime, radium was used to develop the capacity to x-ray injured soldiers on the battlefields of WWI. After her death, scientists used radium to develop the atomic bomb, which in August 1945 destroyed over 150,000 lives at Hiroshima and Nagasaki, Japan. I had not made this connection before: Marie Curie's brave discoveries had been turned to such destructive ends.

In 1985, the U.S. and U.S.S.R. had the power to destroy life on Earth a thousand times over. If this past life connection were true, is this why the soul that was Marie Curie had returned? Distraught that her work had been turned from saving lives to killing hundreds of thousands of people in one instant, had she returned to halt the nuclear arms race? It was a powerful story, the stuff of movies.

I did not care if this story was true or not. I was inspired by Marie Curie's life, by her single-minded devotion to discovering two elements, polonium and radium, that would transform science, medicine, and our understanding of the world and the cosmos.

I asked my chiropractor if he believed in past lives. "I'm open," he said. "Another patient recently told me about a life she thinks I had in ancient Egypt."

Curiously, when I told him I'd been told that he may have been Pierre Curie in a former life, he threw back his head and laughed. "Ha! Let me tell you what happened last weekend. I was attending a conference for chiropractors in San Francisco. On Saturday evening my wife and I had dinner with friends—a chiropractor and his wife—and another couple they knew. During the meal, the wife of the other couple reaches across the table and places her hand on my arm. 'Do you know who you remind me of?' she says with a mischievous smile. 'Pierre Curie!'"

On August 28, I dreamed of the biblical David: young, powerful, strong. In the dream, prophetic words were spoken to my consciousness: "David slew lion, slew lamb." I didn't understand these words, but I remembered the large sepia print that hung above Al's desk in the Senate, the picture of Daniel in the lion's den that served as a reminder to Al that God took care of those who trusted Him.

When I asked the guides about the dream of David, they told me that David represented a new internal masculine that was gaining spiritual strength, unlike the old, task-oriented masculine.

You are affecting people in powerful ways and seeing your own effectiveness. You know where to focus with people so that they are able to move in their perceptions and feelings. Because you have done so much work on integrating the masculine these two years, you can see the feminine inside men waiting to be liberated.

"Tell me more about David, the new masculine."

See how he is not put off by either the lion or the lamb, but learns how to "conquer" his role with both, how to adapt to and make a part of himself both the lion (powerfulness) and the lamb (gentleness). He is learning to be a more complete, adaptive masculine.

"I am ready for the next step in my work. Is there more that I can do to improve my relationships with the men in my outer world?"

Treat each one with delicacy and grace. Do your utmost to respect and prevent harm to anyone.

"I do not want to impose anything on Aaron."

Fear of imposition is a self-defense. Triumph lies in laying down both your sword and your shield. Do not protect yourself from Aaron. His defenses will provide sufficient protection for both of you.

This World.

Acting from a place of love heals relationships, builds friendships, and brings people together. Research has also shown that plants, pets, and babies respond to love.

But this is not all. We can experience love, kindness, and a sense of connection with wild things, too.

Once, after months of feeding at our birdfeeder, a blue jay with a broken wing chirped its way down thirty feet of sidewalk and onto our front steps. My family and I watched from the living room, amazed that the bird had come to us for help. We placed the blue jay in a box and drove twenty miles to a bird rescue center, where they set its wing and, once the wing was healed, let it fly free.

The following year we moved to a remote island in Fiji. One day while I was alone on the island, a Fiji goshawk, small grey-and-pink hawk of the Pacific islands, flew from tree to tree, keeping me in sight as I moved from room to room inside the house. The bird followed me in this manner for three days. A week later I came upon its Fijian name in the dictionary. I was standing at an open window and said its name out loud: "*Latui, latui.*" Within moments the goshawk flashed into a tree in front of me, as though responding to my call, then flew onto the deck railing a few feet from where I stood to peer into my eyes.

In Fiji these experiences became commonplace. Mud dauber wasps, unable to get out of the house once they found their way in, would buzz my head, seemingly asking for assistance. If I pointed to a particular window—one of sixteen in the room—and told a wasp to land there so I could catch it and let it out, the wasp often responded to my request. Likewise, on a number of occasions rain came within minutes after I stepped outside and asked nature to oblige.

In *Messages from Water*, Japanese scientist Masaru Emoto explains this phenomenon at a physical, energetic level. Photographing samples of water, then having individuals pray or feel love in the presence of the water and photographing the samples again, Emoto discovered that the feeling and attitude of love causes water to change from a sludge-like, unorganized mass into beautiful sparkling crystals, no matter how polluted the water was in the first place. Since studying Emoto's work, I've often wondered how love affects the molecules and atoms of our bodies, which are more than 70% water.

My work in the political realm taught me that government workers, congressional staff, and politicians are not immune to the power of love. In truth, we live in a world that hears and feels love and alters its course in response. The implications of this fact are profound. No one and no thing is excluded from the effects of love. Changing the world truly is as simple as that.

12
Love in Action

Within months of meeting with Gore at the Opryland Hotel, I perceived an important internal shift. No longer hounded by my fears, I was moving more boldly in the world. Phyliss' predictions were correct. Much internal debris had washed away, leaving the pool of my awareness clearer and less troubled. I had also set the intention of being a healer, sitting in silence for a period each day to ask for healing for a few friends and family.

As for my neck, I saw that it had led me to Phyliss, to Gore, to Wolfe, and to my chiropractor. It was like a compass directing me where to go next. With this new awareness, I was able to accept its messages with less frustration and follow its course.

I called my heart-centered interactions with political leaders "active loving." Its components were commitment, love, and action. I taught this approach to disarmament and environmental activists and made frequent trips to Washington to meet with Gore, Wolfe, Boner, Sasser, and other members of Congress. My visits were coordinated with the work of national arms control and disarmament organizations. Because of Gore's leadership on arms control issues and his landslide election to the Senate, some national disarmament leaders who knew I was in dialog with Gore and Wolfe considered this to be the most important disarmament work going on in the country.

Gore now sought my advice on key votes, speeches, and

arms control policies, an honor which I found quite humbling. On several occasions he asked me to review his speeches and articles on SDI, the Space Defense Initiative, also known as Star Wars. This proposed multi-billion-dollar "shield" against incoming nuclear weapons would consist of still more nuclear weapons—more money and elaborate games for the Pentagon. Gore now agreed with the Freeze Campaign: Star Wars should not be built.

Early one morning he called to tell me there would be a vote on whether to continue sending federal funds to aid the Nicaraguan contras, the guerrillas who were trying to overthrow the democratically elected, socialist Sandinistas. He wanted to know what I would do. I urged him to vote against aid, which I believed would only prolong the civil war by providing more weapons for more killing. Minutes later, he voted against the funds, and his was the deciding vote. Whether our conversation affected his vote, I did not know.

Under a pseudonym, I wrote an article called "Loving as a Tool for Ending the Arms Race," which appeared in the Re-evaluation Counseling journal *Present Time*. The article detailed my efforts to end racism in Nashville and my disarmament work with members of Congress without naming individuals. The article made its way to activists outside of RC as well, inspiring the creation of two national organizations. In New Jersey's Nuclear Dialog Project, individuals chose a member of Congress or a high-ranking official at the Department of Defense or Department of Energy, learned about this person's interests, and met with him or her to engage in conversation about policies and priorities. In Project Victory, small groups of New Mexico business and community leaders met with generals and other military leaders to discuss strategies for ending the nuclear arms race.

Two years after the article appeared, I was introduced to a top U.S. military leader previously stationed in Germany who, inspired by the article, had initiated walks in the woods with his Soviet counterpart to discuss ways to lessen tensions between the two countries.

On August 28, 1985, Gore delivered a major policy speech on arms control at Nashville's Vanderbilt University. As was typical for Gore's Tennessee speeches, the auditorium was packed. The speech was excellent, outlining in simple terms the complex subject of nuclear arms control. However, I could see how a few changes in the speech would turn a good speech into an even more effective one.

In what I felt was a bold move, I called Peter to tell him I'd like to offer Al feedback on the speech, and that I could do this in person when I attended the National Conference of Common Cause two weeks hence. Peter agreed to put me on Al's schedule.

In mid-September at the appointed time Al met me at his office door and suggested we take a walk. He guided me through Aaron's office to the wide marble corridors of the Russell Senate Office Building.

As we walked, Al turned to me in a hushed voice. "I try to keep conversation to a minimum in my office these days. My office is bugged."

"Bugged?" I whispered, a bit shocked. "By whom? The FBI?"

He nodded, raising his eyebrows.

I wanted to know why, but didn't ask.

We walked in silence for a few moments, passing the stairs and turning right at the corner.

"You heard the Vanderbilt speech?" Al said.

"Yes, it was a very good speech. You have a gift for helping your audience understand a complex subject."

"You had some thoughts?"

"I did. Your intellect and passion about ending the arms race always inspire people. You would inspire them even more by giving them something to do."

"Such as ...?"

"You could encourage them to write letters-to-the-editor of their local newspaper, or call their congressman asking that he or she support efforts in the House that are similar to yours in the Senate. Or talk to their friends and neighbors. They could help educate others about your proposals." Our footsteps resounded in the marble hallways.

"I see." He was pensive, mulling over my thoughts. "Anything else?"

Ahead of us, the corridor opened onto the rotunda.

"You used the analogy of black holes to describe a key concept in your speech. The metaphor is sophisticated, appropriate for a university audience, but it's a negative image. I don't think it sent the message you intended. People will remember your images, so why not leave them with a positive one?"

Al nodded. "Good point." Then he stopped and turned to face me. "I'm giving a speech to the national board of the Sierra Club tonight. I'll incorporate your suggestions."

"Great." I smiled, pleased that my input might be useful to him.

He pointed toward his office. "Let's go back. I have a meeting, and I know Aaron wants to talk with you."

Al called the next day to tell me he had followed my advice and to thank me for my suggestions. "How did you know to do that? They loved my speech, gave me a standing ovation!"

That night I dreamed I was ready to push the button to fire the missiles. I looked for a shelter, but there was none. In the morning the guides told me that the explosion of energy within me was now under my control, but once I pushed the button, there was no retreat or shelter. They added that the day I had said, "Okay, I'm ready!" in frustration had been the game-changer. The rest was merely an unfolding.

In a meeting with Phyliss and Duke several days later, I told them I thought Gore needed to give people a vision of what was possible. Phyliss agreed. "And a way for people to manifest it."

I asked if the book *Vision* by Ken Carey was a good book for him. She said, yes, that plus *Laws of Manifestation.*

Duke was awed by my connections to Gore and Wolfe and my role in helping Gore with his speeches. He said he had never seen this before, how Spirit so clearly was using me.

Phyliss had been worried about me. She had been feeling the absent healing I was doing. "Your guides are completely different from others. Your voices are about absent healing. Yours is a lifestyle; theirs is not. You're living it. You *are* it. Theirs is some other structure. It is similar to how I would describe the disciples around Christ. They were living it, whereas others were trying to understand or doubting his message."

"My difficulty is in trusting the guidance I receive," I told her. "I feel that I know things and have a need to communicate things that are so totally outside of everyone else's experience. My voices say that regardless of the risk I feel, I must communicate what I experience."

"You've got it," Phyliss said. "You don't have a choice. Responsibility is a feeling. You don't need to feel responsible. Trust the messages you are given. With this much of a healer as you are, you need to get that energy out into the world. Don't hold onto it."

Interestingly, Louise Morris had had a dream about Aaron, whom she had never met. In the dream a woman with long black hair approached him in a long hallway in order to give him a message. I asked Phyliss if I should convey the dream to Aaron, and to my surprise she said yes.

When I told the dream to Aaron, he said, "Well, yes, something like that happened to me many years ago."

It was difficult for my mind to make sense of this. Louise had dreamed about an incident that happened to Aaron years ago? The only common thread between Louise and Aaron was me!

The guides told me that Aaron would write me a letter, after two years of no such initiation on his part.

In our next conversation, Aaron asked about my family and

told me about being in the Air Force. He said he occasionally eats with chopsticks.

I laughed. "Important details about your life?"

He laughed, too. "So I guess I don't need to tell you about chopsticks in my letter."

"You're going to write me a letter?" I asked, incredulous.

"I thought yours deserved a response," he said.

Al called and wanted to talk about a teleconference he would initiate soon. He also wanted to discuss the demise of Midgetman, the smaller nuclear missile he and Aaron had been supporting. I suggested a time for a longer conversation.

Subsequent dreams were about Al inviting me to sit at the spiritual table with him. When I asked the guides to explain, they said that I represented to him a hope for the world. *You have suggested that you know where hope lies.*

On February 22, 1986, I dreamed that I was at a banquet where Gore and several others would give after-dinner speeches.

I see Gore before his speech and wish him well. Three people stand up and make predictions about the end of the world. One gives odds of 1:1,863,457 that we can avoid nuclear holocaust. Another gives better odds, based on certain things happening first: 1:500,000. A third person gives odds based on Al taking an active role in negotiating weapons reductions: 183:167. I know when I hear it that the absolutely most important thing I can do is continue to work with him toward averting nuclear holocaust.

That week in a phone conversation with Peter Knight, I accidentally said "I love you," totally beyond my rational mind. Before calling him, I had focused on feeling love, as I always did. The words slipped out, softly, quietly, as he was picking up the phone. It was not my doing at all! I was certain that the guides had decided they would help. Peter did not respond, so I didn't know if he heard me or not.

Love was surely on my mind. I had recently dreamed that I was at a conference where each person stood and said one word. I thought of several possibilities, but when it was my turn, the only word I could think of was "love." I talked about how I was learning new meanings of the word.

Soon after calling Peter, I considered whether to drive 135 miles to Chattanooga to hear Al deliver a speech on "The Future of Tennessee and the Nation." Louise wanted to come, too, so we drove to Chattanooga and stayed the night in a hotel. Listening to Al's speech, I reflected on the dream I'd had about the odds of averting nuclear holocaust and decided that attending the speech was important for all of us—Al, Louise, me, and all whom Al touches.

On April 24, I dreamed: *I am at Al's office, where he and Aaron are working hard to develop a computer program that will give the answers to solving the problems of the nuclear arms race. Al asks the computer, "What is the source of good in the universe?" The computer answers, "Creativity." I realize that the question that needs to be asked next is "What is the source of evil in the universe?" and that the computer's answer will solve the problem they have set for themselves. I want to tell Al, but he's busy. I look for Aaron and discover that he's gone home because it is Saturday.*

I called Peter the next day and learned that their computers had been down. Then I asked the guides about the recent dreams.

A transformation is underway. Witness these changes. Your children are worried about things that no longer worry you. Your father is ill, but you are at peace. You feel that what happens is supposed to happen—there are no accidents. These days you judge very little. You have made a job change with little fear. As for the computers, they represent the mental energy that Al and Aaron work so hard to muster to solve the world's problems. They need your questions. Keep asking! Stop Aaron. Interrupt Al with your questions.

"Should I ask them the question about the source of evil?"

Of course. Why not? Never mind your fear of what they will think. Giving information that feels hard to give has a seminal effect: seeds planted, if watered, become beautiful plants. It feels risky because you fear their judgment. Remember that they love you. Our advice? Let go of the future, then work toward it.

Still later, the guides said: *Teach women how to love this male energy, this person stuck in his patterns. You know how to do it. Show them what to look for. What is needed is a decision not to turn away from the patterns that have crucified us. Being loved, the patterns melt.*

Patterns.

Long before lightning struck my neck, I was aware of the patterns of oppression and how they drive the mechanisms of war. In my first letter to Gore, I had written about my belief that patterns of racism and sexism underlie the nuclear arms race.

Our view of others as different and less than ourselves, which is the essence of racism, keeps us locked into a separatist world view. As well, men's conditioning to choose aggression rather than cooperation, communication, and relationship keeps us funding and deploying the weapons of war. Racism and sexism, plus greed, are the patterns that crucify us.

The guides asked me to teach what I was learning about how to love the person inside the pattern. I had written about this work anonymously and taught the concepts in Re-evaluation Counseling classes and at international conferences such as Common Boundary. I was reluctant to share the ideas more publicly out of deference to those who were still in positions of power within the U.S. government.

In RC terms, a pattern (or distress pattern) is the result of people being hurt. The theory states that we humans are naturally loving, vibrantly alive, and intelligent. Hurtful experiences cause us to behave otherwise, obscuring our natural state of being. The person is not the pattern. When we see a person acting out of anger, fear, or despair, we know that they have been hurt; this is also true when a person behaves in any way other than loving and intelligent. Listening to such a person with loving attention allows the hurt to be released.

The theory held true in my work with people in positions of power. Each time I related with love and kindness to the person inside the pattern, it was the person that responded, not the pattern. Understanding patterns helped me to see why love is the answer.

13
Rainbows over Reykjavik

In May 1986, the thought came to me that I would become director of the Nuclear Weapons Freeze Campaign in Washington.

Move to Washington? Direct the Freeze Campaign? It seemed an outrageous idea. I talked to the guides, who said, yes, it's true. I would move to Washington and direct the Freeze Campaign.

I was skeptical. For starters, the position of executive director was not open. More importantly, my children were ensconced in a school with over 100 international students and a Korean teacher who was helping them learn English. Ron was thriving in his work, receiving recognition for his leadership of Quality Circles at Nissan. And my mother and her husband, Joe, lived just fifteen minutes away from us, so that I could see her often and offer support. I decided that the insight might be a bright idea, but it wasn't a practical one.

On my travels to Washington to meet with members of Congress and national Freeze and Common Cause staff, I stayed with Marilyn, a woman I'd met through the Freeze Campaign who graciously opened her home for my visits.

Four weeks after my insight, Marilyn and I were drinking tea in her upstairs studio when she said, "Have you heard? Jane left the Freeze Campaign and they're looking for a new director."

This took me aback. "You're kidding! Jane has left?" I told her about my thought that I would become the next director.

Marilyn set her cup down, and her eyes lit up. "What a great idea! You're the perfect person for the job. They need someone with a fresh perspective and a record of success in working with Congress. And your grassroots experience is excellent."

I shook my head. "I don't see how I can do it. My family is very happy where they are."

"We need you, no doubt about that," Marilyn insisted. "I hope you'll seriously consider applying."

It seemed too complicated for my family, but I found the idea intriguing and exciting.

When Ron and I talked about this possibility, he didn't hesitate. "If you want the job, you should go for it. Things will work out for us to move to Washington."

"Are you sure? It would be an enormous change for our family."

"Yes, I'm sure. It's a great opportunity."

I was grateful for Ron's support, and for that of the guides. Still, the task of moving felt daunting. If I were to take the job, I would need everything to line up behind the decision. I told the guides in no uncertain terms that everything would have to be smooth and easy.

You have our blessings and heartfelt thanks for taking this on and for receiving us one-and-a-half years ago. You have made astute preparation for the job ahead. It is yours for the asking. Thank you from all of us.

Such confidence. Could it be that simple?

Ron and I decided to wait to tell Amy and David that we were considering the move until the hiring committee had requested an interview. The four of us had visited D.C. on vacation, and the children knew I went there often to work, but we had never mentioned the possibility of moving there.

One night over dinner Amy looked up, a bright smile on her eight-year-old face. "I'd like to live in Washington, D.C."

Ron and I exchanged glances. "Why would you like to do that?" he asked.

Amy shrugged, still grinning. "I'd just like to."

So: Ron was supportive, and Amy was interested. Within

a couple of weeks of my applying for the job, Ron had made contact with a consulting firm in northern Virginia that was interested in hiring him. And when I told my mother I had applied for the Freeze position, she said that she and Joe would follow us to Washington. It sounded good to her.

The call came a month later. I was one of the top three candidates. Could I come to D.C. in two weeks? I was excited and spent the time reflecting on what I thought I could bring to the job.

In Washington, while waiting to meet with the hiring committee, I encountered the other two candidates in the waiting room, both of whom I knew from my work with the national Freeze. Both were male; both had strengths quite different from my own. Al Gore had written me a glowing letter of recommendation, which impressed the hiring committee, as did my organizing work in Tennessee and my commitment to conflict resolution and peacemaking. I learned during the interview that the Freeze staff were feeling demoralized because funds had dropped precipitously, over twenty people had been laid off, and plans were underway for a merger with SANE, an older national peace organization.

I returned to Nashville. The wait seemed interminable, but was actually about three months. I wondered why the hiring committee was taking so long, when the guides and my intuition told me that the job belonged to me.

Impressed with my grassroots, lobbying, and management experience, the Freeze board offered me the job. They liked that I had ideas about how to heal divisions within the peace movement and how to work with a staff that was discouraged and disillusioned.

Once the board had notified me of their decision, I spoke again with the guides, who offered advice they said would be crucial to my success:

The cost of not trusting your own heart is greater because of the times we're in. We expect you to trust it at all times. It will move things much faster.

My move to Washington was still three weeks away when the chair of the Freeze board called to request that I attend the Reagan-Gorbachev Summit in Iceland. The overnight flight to Reykjavik would depart from New York in three days, so I needed to book my flight immediately. I was thrilled. I had never dreamed I might attend an arms control summit.

I dug excitedly through my desk to find my passport. To my dismay, it had expired. "How can I possibly go?" I asked Ron. "No one gets a passport in three days."

"You could call Gore's office," he suggested. "You have that relationship. If anyone can help you, they can."

I phoned Peter Knight to tell him my predicament. He checked his schedule. "We can do it if you fly to D.C. first. I'll meet you at National Airport and take you to the Congressional Passport Office. We'll need two hours to get it done."

I booked a morning flight for Thursday, October 9, with a four-hour layover in D.C., which would continue on to New York's JFK Airport in the afternoon.

Peter met me at the airport and drove me into the city, where I filed a passport application, my photo was taken, and we waited. The passport was ready in an hour and a half. We drove back to the airport; Peter hugged me and wished me good luck.

In New York I met the rest of the peace delegation: three staff from SANE including Executive Director John Fortin, plus six members of the newly formed Women for a Meaningful Summit. The flight was crowded, the excitement palpable. It appeared that the majority of those on board were traveling to the summit.

Reykjavik, Iceland's capital and largest city, lay on a peninsula under fresh, pale skies. Everything was white and blue—the rocks, the water, the sky, even the buildings. Reykjavik is the northernmost capital of a sovereign state, but the warm waters of the Gulf Stream soften its winters. For the October summit, the days would be sunny and crisp, the nights cold.

Over 10,000 international press and other observers had arrived, seeking accommodation in a city of 90,000. SANE's Washington staff had arranged for the SANE contingent and me to stay with an Icelandic family, who greeted us warmly. The mother, father, and ten-year-old son served as our guide to the city and plied us with sumptuous food day and night. When we returned late in the evening after meeting with other peace delegations, hot coffee and a tray piled with chocolate croissants, cake, and other goodies awaited us. We felt welcome in this home and in Reykjavik, where everything seemed to sparkle in the sun.

We would be in Reykjavik for three days, with negotiations taking place on October 11 and 12. The U.S. delegation, headed by President Reagan and Secretary of State George Schultz, arrived the same day we did. Premier Gorbachev and the Soviet delegation arrived that night on a ship that docked in the harbor. The negotiators would meet at Hofdi House, the former French consulate that was viewable from across the harbor.

The next morning we sighted Gorbachev from afar. He and Reagan stood on the steps of Hofdi House, about to go inside. They shook hands and smiled for the press. The sky over Reykjavik was clear, and a brilliant rainbow spread over their heads. It was one of five rainbows we would see those three days.

The feeling on the streets and in the hotel foyers was one of excitement and optimism. Everyone agreed it was remarkable that these two leaders would talk about reducing their nuclear arsenals. The U.S. media made much of the fact that Gorbachev arrived in Iceland under the halo of a rainbow.

Our peace delegation issued press releases twice a day, commenting on the negotiations and calling for a halt to U.S. and Soviet nuclear test explosions as a way to slow the arms race. John Fortin and I requested meetings with Soviet Minister of Foreign Affairs Eduard Shevardnadze and Secretary Schultz in order to present the position of the American people. I felt it was a bold request, given the importance of their work there.

The international media was interested in our position and contacted us for numerous interviews, both for their newspapers back home and for Icelandic television. We held a press conference, which was attended by European and Japanese reporters. The U.S. media did not show up. Apparently the U.S. press did not consider it a story that our country's peace movement leaders had come to Iceland.

The official U.S. delegation did not respond to our request for a meeting, but we received a note from Anatoly Dobrynin, Secretary of the Central Committee of the Communist Party, inviting John and me to meet with him on the Soviet ship. Soviet Ambassador to the U.S. from 1962 to 1986, Dobrynin had played a crucial role during the Cuban Missile Crisis and the terms of six U.S. presidents. I considered it a great honor that he had invited us to meet with him.

At 7:30 the next morning John and I took a taxi to the ship, where two Soviet officials greeted us and led us to a small pine-paneled cabin. Secretary Dobrynin, a large man, gray-haired and balding, sat at a metal table smoking a cigarette. The table was surrounded on two sides by a red vinyl-covered booth. Chairs had been placed for John and me beside the table, facing the secretary.

Dobrynin welcomed us in English and offered us cigarettes, which we declined. "Would you like coffee?" I rarely drank coffee, but I accepted. An attendant stepped forward to pour coffee into waiting cups.

"Thank you for seeing us," John began. "We are honored to have the opportunity to meet with you."

Dobrynin nodded from behind round-rimmed glasses, tapping ashes into a glass ashtray. "Of course. We are happy to have the conversation with you. We follow your peace movement in the United States."

John described the Nuclear Freeze proposal, the resolution that had passed Congress, and the movement that was invigorating our country. "Over 80% of the American people support an end to the arms race."

"We are aware of this," Dobrynin said. "Still your president does not change his behavior. Perhaps you have suggestions for us, what we can do to persuade your president to negotiate reductions in nuclear weapons."

"A nuclear test ban would be a good first step toward halting the construction of new weapons," I said. "We think that 50,000 nuclear weapons between the U.S. and the Soviet Union is quite enough."

He nodded almost imperceptibly. "We agree with you. For us, it is much more difficult to continue to build weapons. We spend all our resources trying to keep up with the U.S., when we need these funds to solve our problems at home. Our people are very poor. Building more nuclear weapons is a great strain on our country."

"If the Soviet Union stopped testing, this would encourage the U.S. to stop as well," said John.

Dobrynin snuffed out his cigarette, considering John's point. "It is a travesty that we continue in this way."

I thought of Nikita Khrushchev's statement years earlier, as premier of the U.S.S.R. *No one will be able to see the difference between capitalist and communist ashes.*

We chatted briefly about a total freeze on testing, producing and deploying nuclear weapons. Dobrynin thought it unlikely that Reagan would ever agree to this. At a lull in the conversation, he thanked us for coming and signaled a man stationed at the door to escort us off the ship. John and I left feeling pleased with the meeting. Photos taken on that day showed both of us beaming.

I was amazed that Dobrynin had asked for our advice. Back home, conservatives often charged the peace movement with being Communist sympathizers, toeing the Soviet line. It was laughable to me, as it was far from the truth, so I was fascinated that the Soviets were following *us*. In an odd sort of way, the nation that we'd been told did not listen to its own people appeared to be listening to the people of the United States to help set its policy.

The Soviet leaders, of course, were not just talking to leaders of the U.S. peace movement. They were talking to members of Congress, Reagan administration officials, every person they thought could help them figure out how to work with the U.S. administration. All of this was taking place in an atmosphere where the U.S. government was not listening to its own people. Instead, they listened to Department of Defense officials, firms like General Electric and Halliburton that built nuclear weapons, and scientists on the government payroll.

Conservatives claimed that the Soviets were ahead of the U.S. in the nuclear arms race, but this charge obscured the facts. The Soviet Union's Intercontinental Ballistic Missiles (ICBM's) were larger and heavier than ours, but the U.S. had a much-advanced technology, which translated into more accuracy and greater speed.

Late that morning we peace delegates stood across the bay from Hofdi House holding banners in the chill arctic air, calling for an end to U.S.-U.S.S.R. nuclear testing. I hoped that we were harbingers of a spring to come; that, indeed, one day Congress and the administration might embrace a test ban.

In the negotiations Reagan raised the issues of human rights, Soviet dissidents, and the Soviet invasion of Afghanistan, while Gorbachev insisted that the summit focus solely on nuclear weapons. Gorbachev was intent on major weapons reductions for at least two reasons: first, the economic hardship caused by extravagant weapons spending necessary for the U.S.S.R. to keep up with the U.S. and, second, the enormous damage and clean-up expense caused by the nuclear disaster at the Chernobyl nuclear power plant, which had occurred just six months earlier.

On the final day of the summit, news broke that a significant reduction in nuclear weapons was on the table. Gorbachev was suggesting the elimination of all nuclear weapons within a decade; we were unclear of the U.S. position at this point. We peace delegates went to the White Hotel, where members of the press had gathered to wait for a statement. They paced the hallways, slumped in chairs in the lobbies. The air was taut like a wire, ready—like this story—to break. We overheard them. "Won't this be something?" one said. "The hottest story of the decade." Meanwhile, the "deal" grew; rumor had it that the number of weapons to be dismantled was huge.

Back home, the conservatives were going crazy. News reports echoed their distress: "We cannot trust the Soviets!"

Icelandic TV announced that George Shultz would hold a briefing. Everyone gathered around television sets in the main lobby and hallways.

Shultz's face appeared, looking very sober, tired, disheartened. We almost got this, he said, but it slipped away. We almost got that, but it slipped away, too. We almost agreed to get rid of half our nuclear weapons on both sides. But none of this happened.

Everyone was disappointed, not the least the reporters. The press, the peace delegates, and George Shultz had almost tasted victory. On the flight home, many members of the press got drunk, some sulking, others carousing loudly. One could feel their disappointment that this story didn't end right. The fish had gotten away, and the media was bummed out.

Although the talks collapsed, leaving both sides empty-handed, it was an enormous breakthrough, essentially heralding the end of the Cold War. The Reagan-Gorbachev Reykjavik Summit would set the stage for the Intermediate-Range Nuclear Forces Treaty to be signed one year later in December 1987, as well as future agreements over the next few years.

The U.S. media's refusal to cover the peace movement or to report on polls showing 80% of Americans wanting an end to the nuclear arms race bordered on criminal. By not allowing the public to know about the work that was being done by citizens around the world to end the nuclear arms race, the media disempowered those who were looking for a sign of hope. They did not do this out of ignorance. They were, after all, the "free press."

Two weeks later, as I loaded my car for Washington, D.C., I pondered the summit and what these new developments would mean for my job as executive director of the Nuclear Weapons Freeze Campaign. I was arriving just as the possibility of reducing nuclear weapons was opening up. I would be in Washington by myself for a while, settling into an apartment until Ron and I could shop for a house and move the family to D.C.

I was excited to have this job that fate had handed me. It was a very difficult time for the Freeze, which had shrunk to a staff of ten from its previous thirty-five. On my first day, a staff member told me that they referred to the director's office as "the black hole, because the former director could never seem to get her head above water, and things that went in there never came out."

The Freeze Campaign was on its last legs financially. Foundations and donors who were committed to the grassroots network had helped keep the Freeze afloat. They were glad that someone new was at the helm and told me privately that they wanted to provide support so that the Freeze would be strong going into the merger; they did not want SANE to "take over" the Freeze.

The merger promised to bring together the country's two strongest peace organizations: SANE with its membership base, research team, and phone banks; and the Freeze with its grassroots groups and success in passing over 200 Freeze resolutions in city councils and state legislatures. The outcome seemed inevitable, given the Freeze's financial situation. I had the impression that some SANE staff, knowing the weakened state of the Freeze national office, were indeed looking forward to taking over the grassroots network.

At the National Freeze Conference, six weeks after I assumed the position of executive director, several hundred Freeze delegates voted to merge with SANE in a show of solidarity and hope for the future of the peace movement. Shortly after the merger vote, a committee composed of board members of the two organizations decided that John and I would be co-directors. To resolve any differences between us, the new board would hire a president who would be given final decision-making power.

Until the board could hire a president, John and I were to co-manage the merged organization. John was given purview over the power center of the organization—political issues and financial management—while I would be in charge of grassroots and communications. The management structure made sense from the perspective that John Fortin had many years of political and financial management experience. From another perspective, however, the structure was detrimental to the Freeze half of the merged organization. Without a hand in the finances, I was unable to make important decisions about the programs I managed. John had his ideas; I had mine. Understandably, the staff felt uncertain about lines of authority and was tossed about between us. In addition, several former Freeze and SANE staff members had ties to the local Communist party, and these individuals were willing to pull out the stops to further their own agenda. It was the cloak and dagger that Phyliss had warned me about, conflict in the realm of peace.

In August 1987, John declined an invitation to join a U.S.-U.S.S.R. Peace Cruise on the Volga River and asked if I would like to go in his place. I had traveled across Siberia at the end of my Peace Corps stint in Thailand and was delighted to have a chance to return to the Soviet Union for the first time in twenty years. I was also grateful for the respite from the management struggles.

The purpose of the voyage was to discuss ways for Americans and Soviets to work together to end the nuclear arms race at a time when it appeared the Cold War would soon be over. I would serve as resource person on the cruise, making presentations in workshops alongside Soviet counterparts, including the head of the Soviet Peace Committee. Our ship would follow the Don and Volga Rivers from Rostov-on-Don to Kazan, stopping at Saratov, Ulyanovsk, and Volgograd. From Kazan we would travel by train to Leningrad. On the cruise would be 130 Americans and 50 Soviet officials and journalists.

U.S. cruise participants flew to Moscow and spent what was left of the night at the Hotel Rossiya, located beside Red Square. A true Moscow monument, twelve stories high and encompassing an enormous city block, the hotel was so large and complex that one could lose their way and wander for hours. I did, in fact, get lost on more than one occasion.

We were in Moscow one day and two nights, admiring the brightly painted domes of St. Basil's Cathedral and exploring the streets around Red Square. Our first day in Moscow, a young couple, just wedded, crossed the square looking as happy and innocent as any newly married couple anywhere. The bride wore a white wedding dress and veil; the wedding party sported red sashes. This was a photo worth taking: life went on in the Soviet Union in ways similar to life back home.

The following day we boarded buses for a tour of the city, then flew to Rostov-on-Don, the beginning point of our cruise. Once we settled into our cabins on the ship, we gathered again to tour Rostov's downtown area, factories, and park with its monument to World War II. Between stops, the guide on the bus paused to say, "You have come in peace, and we love you. Thank you for working for peace."

When we returned to the ship, several hundred Russians were waiting for us on the dock, waving peace flags and cheering our arrival. We cheered and waved back. An American folk singer played the guitar and sang the Russian children's peace song, *"Poost vsegda boodyet sonseh"* ("May there always be sunshine") to the smiles and laughter of those who had gathered to see us off.

Organizers of the cruise had told us to bring small gifts to exchange—pens, chewing gum, and postcards of our home town. After encountering several Russians and exchanging gifts, I found myself looking into the face of a woman in her early forties whose intense brown eyes and short doeskin hair were similar to my own. She introduced herself as Elena and her children as Natasha and Yuri. All three were waving tiny flags with "peace" written in Russian and English. My Russian was meager, as was their English, so we passed my dictionary between us.

"Do you have children?" Elena asked in Russian.

"Yes, a girl and a boy, ten and eleven."

She clasped her children, one with each arm. "Mine are eight and thirteen."

Natasha, the older of the two, beamed at me. She looked no more than ten years old with her straight, cropped hair and boyish clothes. Yuri's expression was serious, his cheeks cherubic and rosy.

"What kind of work do you do?" I asked Elena.

"I work in *fa-bri-ca*." She nodded at each syllable.

It took me a few moments to remember. "Ah, factory."

Elena broke into a smile, and all three nodded emphatically. "And you?"

"I work for world peace, in Washington, D.C."

"O-o-oh! World peace." She repeated the Russian words, *miru mir.* "We want peace very much." Then she leaned close and spoke in a hushed voice. "Do you believe in God?" When I didn't understand, she showed me the Russian word for "God" in the dictionary.

"Yes, I do." Her question surprised me, as the Soviet government had suppressed religion since the beginning of communist party rule.

"Do you go to church?" Elena continued.

I nodded. "Yes, do you?"

"No church, but I believe."

When the ship's dinner bell tolled, Elena and her children left, saying they would return before our 7:30 p.m. departure.

Later, from the deck, I saw them waiting for me amid the gathering crowd. Elena caught sight of me and waved enthusiastically. On the dock I gave her a pair of silver filigree earrings and her eyes filled with tears. She took a small figurine from her purse—a dancing Cossack— placed it in my hand, and hugged me. *"Mui, droozhya,"* she said, "We're friends, you and I."

A band of musicians began playing Russian folk songs as the crowd pressed into us. We hugged again, and I boarded the ship. I waved goodbye as the ship pulled from the dock.

At every stop along the river hundreds of Russians greeted us, each person bearing postcards, flowers, stamps, or enameled lapel pins; each one handing us gifts and declaring us friends. As well, every dock was lively and gay with gymnastic performances, dances, and music. Although I had traversed the country and spent several days in Moscow in 1967, the Peace Cruise was my first experience of meeting and talking to the people of the Soviet Union. In 1967 almost everyone had been afraid to talk to us; everyone was closed off.

On the ship and in the port cities our conversations inevitably led back to World War II, where twenty million lives—one-fourth of the entire Soviet population—were lost to Hitler's forces. Every family lost a husband, brother, or father. "This is why we want peace so badly," they said. "This is why we are so happy to meet you and be your friend. This is why we love you, because you work for peace." My father, my schools, and the media had firmly impressed upon me that the Soviets were our enemy. Now I found myself interacting one-on-one with dozens of Russians, each one placing a gift in my hand, each one wanting to be my friend.

Early in the cruise the ship docked near a beach for a play about Neptune, God of the Sea, and a picnic of hamburgers, hotdogs, and potato salad. I was chosen to be Neptune's wife, complete with long turquoise cape and tinseled crown. We players arrived on the beach by rowboat, where an appreciative audience waited for Neptune, his messenger, three servants, two cooks, and me. Neptune issued a proclamation: "May peace prevail on Earth! May this U.S.-Soviet Peace Cruise help to bring peace to the planet!" Scrolls containing the proclamation were handed out to the participants. Then we were called to the picnic grounds, where a game of volleyball and the barbecue ensued.

Our next stop was Volgograd, formerly known as Stalingrad, where the Russians suffered over one million casualties against Hitler's forces, considered to be the turning point of World War II in Europe. Hitler lost as many forces to the Russians, his Nazi soldiers suffering through the bitter winter without food and shelter, many trapped inside the city. Our tour of Volgograd took us to a section of the city that had been left in ruins as a reminder of the costs of war, and to a war park with an imposing 279-foot-tall statue named "The Motherland Calls." At the time of its construction, it was the largest sculpture in the world.

Later we waited in the rain to meet factory workers at the end of their shift. Swinging from the top of the building were banners with slogans in Russian, red letters on white: "Long Live the People" and "Long Live the Revolution." The air smelled of oil, grease, and dirt. The rain spattered my umbrella and soaked the hem of my dress; my shoes filled with water.

The factory issued a shrill whistle, followed by an explosion of workers who spilled out the metal gates. Three older women in babushkas, their faces round and doughy, walked toward me. I approached them and spoke to the woman in front, who wore a shabby blue and beige cotton dress.

"I am an American. I give this to you for peace," I said in Russian, handing her a blue button that read "Mir-Peace -U.S.-U.S.S.R." with an image of our white ship.

Her eyes squinched tight to hold back tears as the other two women gathered close to look. Slowly she unfastened a rhinestone pin from over her breast and pressed it into my hand. *"Mir, mir, droog drooga,"* she said, "Peace, peace, we are friends, you and I."

I thought this might be her most prized possession and was deeply touched. This moment, her hand in mine, with the pin resting in my palm, left an impression that did not fade in the coming weeks. An egg was cracking inside me, gently breaking open the shell of my beliefs and feelings about the Soviet Union and her people.

As our ship continued up the Volga River, the Soviets pointed out the buildings that housed each city's peace committee. The government had provided the peace committees with the former homes of nobles: elegant buildings with velvet curtains and cut-glass chandeliers. I learned that peace was not a suspicious or dirty word. Everyone talked about peace, longed for it. Banners calling for peace hung from buildings in many cities. Having lost so many people in World War II, and with the war fought on their soil, the Russians knew deeply the devastation of war. They repeatedly told us that they longed for a time when they could stop building weapons of mass destruction in order to rebuild their country. In workshops on the ship, I discovered that the U.S. and Soviet peace leaders were in agreement on steps to reversing the arms race.

One-on-one, people told me that the society was changing rapidly. Taking photos was now permitted, unlike in 1967. Thousands of small groups had begun meeting in the mid-1980s in living rooms throughout the country, talking about what needed to change. Ideas were shared about what would hasten the transformation of the U.S.S.R. into a democratic country. Everyone saw it coming—indeed, had seen it coming for several years. It was too late to turn back, they said. Gorbachev knew about this and was allowing it.

In Leningrad, we visited Piskaryevskoye Memorial Cemetery, which commemorates the 872-day siege of Leningrad during WW II. Over one million civilians lost their lives during the siege and evacuations; over one million Red Army soldiers also died, and 2.5 million soldiers were wounded or became ill.

A small group of Soviet veterans saw us with our peace buttons and asked who we were. They wore jackets decorated with ribbons and medals; their thick gray hair and rugged faces reminded me of my grandfather. They told us proudly that they had fought in the trenches alongside Americans. When I told them that my father was a pilot during the war, four of them gathered around me to touch my cheeks and tell me that we could be friends.

Organizers of the cruise had asked the U.S. resource persons to give speeches in each city we visited along the river. Most of these speeches were impersonal and full of platitudes. As a newcomer to the national peace movement, I was not asked to speak until Leningrad, our last stop. As I prepared my speech, I thought about my experiences along the river, the gracious welcome at each city and the overwhelming kindness of our Soviet hosts. I felt inadequate to this task, but I knew it was important to speak from the heart and to the hearts of my audience, so I crafted a speech about the people we had met, the generosity we had experienced, and the friendships we had made. I told them about the young boy who gave me a cancelled postage stamp in a Ulyanovsk park, the woman who gave me the change I needed to ride a city bus in Kazan, the woman in Volgograd who pressed her rhinestone pin into my palm. I said that this was what makes for peace. As I spoke, I saw the eyes of one of the cruise organizers light up. He shook his head and mouthed to me, "Why have we put you off till last?" The audience applauded my words. They smiled and cried and afterwards thanked me profusely.

We returned to Moscow, where we had requested a meeting with President Gorbachev. Although he had met with groups from the U.S. on several occasions, he was unavailable at the time of our visit, so we met with First Vice Chairman of the Supreme Soviet, Pyotr Demichev. Eight U.S. delegates filed into the small conference room and seated ourselves along one side of a long narrow table, facing Soviet officials.

The U.S. delegates talked about how happy they were that the Soviets were willing to negotiate an end to the arms race. There was much praise for the Soviet position, but no one asked the Soviets for anything. This felt like a wasted opportunity to me.

As luck had it, I was sitting in the center of the narrow table, directly across from Demichev. "Vice Chairman," I said, "we are interested in a complete ban on nuclear testing. As you and we know, both countries halted testing in the atmosphere, under water, and on land with the signing of the 1963 Partial Test Ban Treaty by Khrushchev and Kennedy. What we need now is an end to nuclear testing underground."

The vice chairman was smiling at me. "Yes, of course."

"If the Soviets would stop testing, it would give the U.S. an incentive to do the same. We ask that the Soviet Union take this step."

"Very well said." He nodded to me, then to an official sitting to his left.

After the meeting he came around the table to take my hand in both of his. "The Americans are lucky to have you."

I was not flattered by this. I knew that his comment was stirred by my willingness to speak.

As we headed back to the Rossiya Hotel to pack for the trip home, I stared out the bus window and thought about the people I'd met and the experiences I'd had. I saw that leadership would be needed in the U.S. to end nuclear testing. The idea for my future work became clear to me: I would coordinate a campaign to end nuclear testing.

Returning to Washington, I shifted my focus to ending U.S. and Soviet nuclear test explosions—nuclear testing—a goal that many thought was achievable. When they heard about my intention to form a coalition, Parliamentarians for Global Action, a nonprofit organization of legislators and parliamentarians from around the world, and International Physicians for the Prevention of Nuclear War asked me to join them. They were preparing for a meeting of the 118 delegates to the 1963 Partial Test Ban Treaty (PTBT), to be convened at the United Nations in January 1991. The purpose of the conference was to consider amending the PTBT into a comprehensive test ban (CTB) that would prohibit testing in all environments, including underground. Under my leadership, the U.S. CTB Coalition would become the U.S. branch of the international campaign, coordinating its efforts with grassroots groups in hundreds of cities and towns throughout the country.

I continued to work with Gore and Wolfe and other members of Congress. John Fortin and I met with Soviet Ambassador Yuri Dubinin, who said, "What else can we Soviets do? We are trying to do everything you in the peace movement tell us to do." When we urged the Soviets to stop nuclear weapons testing unilaterally, Dubinin said they would give this their utmost consideration.

In October 1987, the Berlin Wall came down, in a collective moment of heart-opening and hope. Many political analysts were certain that the Soviet Union would dissolve as well. I wanted to talk with the Soviets I had met on the cruise, but relationships between our two countries were still extremely tense, and communication nearly impossible. The CIA had a file on me as a leader in the peace movement, and phone calls to the U.S.S.R. would most certainly be added to my dossier.

During this time, I had a dream that a powerful entity or spirit had visited me on several occasions, leaving me feeling warm, loving, loved, and encircled with powerful energy. In the dream, three of my friends were skeptical about this spirit's existence. We went to an auditorium where the spirit sat at the front, beaming energy and light at us. He sent three white doves, one to each of my friends, and the doves kissed each one on the face. Then the spirit left.

I awoke feeling overwhelmingly blessed, as though I had visited heaven.

Things might have been hopeful and positive in the world at large, but the management situation at SANE-Freeze was untenable. As soon as I made a decision, obtained John's agreement, and announced the decision to the staff, John reversed my decision and communicated the new decision to everyone. I understood that he was used to being in charge, but the staff was furious, and rightly so. I met with individual staff to offer my support, and we held meetings with the entire staff to try to resolve the problems, but they were of little help. Throughout, I struggled to keep my equanimity.

The hiring process for the position of president had begun, which offered hope that the management issues would be resolved. Surely, one final decision maker would be better than two. As the process proceeded, two final candidates emerged: Rev. William Sloane Coffin, a popular activist-minister from New York City; and Rep. Bob Edgar, a former congressman from Pennsylvania. Both were progressive and had ideas in line with the goals of SANE-Freeze.

John and I sat on the hiring committee along with other staff and board members from the two halves of the merged organization. Maureen Essay, a former SANE board member, now on the SANE-Freeze Board and a friend of Bill Coffin's, sat in on the deliberations, without a vote. I didn't believe it was right for someone close to one of the candidates to do this, but I didn't protest. We interviewed both candidates—both were impressive—and afterwards a committee member asked us to indicate by straw poll whom we would vote for, given what we knew thus far. Another round of interviews would follow, but this woman thought a straw poll was a good idea. I was leaning toward supporting Coffin and said so. I did not realize at the time that this poll had another, unstated purpose.

A few days later Rev. Coffin saw me on the street and asked to talk to me. I was headed to my car and invited him to sit in the front seat.

"I want to thank you for voting for me," he said.

I was stunned into silence. How could he know this, when the deliberations of the committee were to be held in strict confidence? I nodded and said nothing. It seemed likely that Maureen had told Bill Coffin about my vote. The hiring committee would meet again later in the week, and I resolved to ask about the breach of confidentiality. When we gathered on Thursday evening, I told the committee what Rev. Coffin had said to me and asked how he could know this. Maureen was irate.

At the SANE-Freeze board meeting the following day, two board members from the SANE side of the organization took me to task for "inappropriate behavior" in the committee meeting. They were not members of the hiring committee. Another confidence had been broken.

Unfortunately, I did not stand up to them. I did not tell the entire board about Rev. Coffin knowing my straw vote. I did not want to lose my job, and I knew my job was at stake. It was a moment I regretted for a long time. I replayed this moment on my mental tape recorder, redoing the meeting in my head for weeks afterward. I wished I had spoken plainly: "It is not I who has acted inappropriately. Bill Coffin knew about my straw vote, which I had shared with the hiring committee in confidence. We had sworn ourselves to confidentiality. Who told him what I said? This is what we need to find out."

Why didn't I do this? After much soul searching, I knew that my fear of speaking up went back to my childhood, where my father had threatened to kill me if I told anyone he was molesting me. I had felt guilty then, as though I was doing something wrong. But he was the guilty one. *His* behavior was inappropriate, not mine.

I learned at the board meeting that Bob Edgar had withdrawn, leaving Coffin as the only candidate. Coffin's hiring was assured. Two months later I found out that someone had called Edgar the same week that Coffin had spoken to me about my vote. The purpose of the call? To tell Edgar that the votes were stacked against him and he could not win. The tragedy was not lost on me: Once I was aware that the hiring process had been subverted, I would have changed my vote.

By raising the issue of confidentiality in the hiring committee, I had risked my job in order to assure that the hiring of a president was handled fairly, and that the new president and his relationships with staff and board members were in integrity. Bob Edgar would have been such a president, one without a special relationship with John, board members, or myself.

Maureen, John, and others from the former SANE half of the organization rallied to force me out. Bob Edgar took the position of executive director of the nonprofit organization Committee for National Security and asked me to join him. He told me I could bring the CTB Coalition with me. I resigned from SANE-Freeze and joined Bob at CNS.

The Enemy.

In 1971, the cartoon character Pogo, looking out over garbage and debris that humans had tossed into the Okefenokee

Swamp, said, "We have met the enemy, and he is us." Printed on posters shortly thereafter, the phrase quickly became popular in American culture.

Adults had taught me from an early age that the Russians were our enemy. I was cognizant of the dynamics of U.S.-Soviet relations and the threat communism represented to capitalist interests. I understood that the leaders of both countries had values to maintain and countries to protect. But no one had said the Russian people were like us, like me. On the cruise I met hundreds of Russians—families with children, factory workers, school girls, grandmothers, gymnasts, WW II veterans, Peace Committee members and staff—everyone longing for peace. The egg cracking inside me was giving birth to a new understanding about the role governments play, and a heartfelt connection to the Soviet people.

For years I had also encountered the media's blackout of coverage of the peace movement, their decision to ignore the global effort involving millions of people working for peace; their refusal to let others know that, year after year, thousands of people were committing civil disobedience and being arrested at the Nevada Test Site and many other nuclear weapons facilities.

The U.S. government and the media labeled those working for peace as "peaceniks," suggesting a kinship with the counterculture "beatniks" of the 1950s and Russia's orbiting "sputnik" of the 1960s. We were marginalized and called unpatriotic—supposedly duped by the Soviets—even though among our ranks were former U.S. nuclear bomb scientists and high-ranking, retired military personnel. I often wondered what could be more patriotic than peace.

I was also seeing on a day-to-day basis the integrity—or lack of it—of certain members of the peace movement. I knew I had participated in my own way by not speaking up. My timidity and fear of losing my job had won out over telling the truth. Gandhi had said, "Be the change you wish to see in the world." Those of us working for peace were struggling to do just that and sometimes failing.

There was so much to understand about making peace.

Certainly love, kindness, compassion, and integrity were a part of the answer.

I pondered the question: Who and what are the enemies of peace?

14
Dinner in a Yurt

Gore called me in early 1987. He was deciding whether or not to run for president. What did I think? Should he run? He was concerned about his family and the timing. He intended to run at some point, but was this the right time? At thirty-nine years old, Gore would be the youngest serious candidate to run for U.S. president since John F. Kennedy.

I listened carefully then told him I thought the American people were hungry for the truth and for a leader with vision, perspective, and an integrated strategy. If he decided to run, I urged him to trust himself totally. "Don't let others sway you from what you know is right," I said. "Trust your own thinking and your own heart."

He thanked me for this advice and hung up. On April 11, he announced his candidacy. I made a list of ideas and sent it to Peter to pass on to him:

- Articulate your vision as a holistic, integrated approach.
- A world without nuclear weapons, and how we could get there using your approach; how we would change our relationship with the Soviets. You would be an excellent match for Gorbachev.
- A protected environment.
- Truth and honesty in government, modeled at the top.
- A focus on building community at the local level.
- Support for local and state initiatives.

The *New York Times* described him as "a long shot for the presidential nomination, but many believed he could provide a natural complement for any of the other candidates: a young, attractive, moderate vice presidential nominee from the South." *Washington Monthly* also called Gore a "long, long shot" for the White House.

Gore stumped throughout the rest of the year preparing for the Iowa caucuses and New Hampshire. He expected to win the Southern Democratic primaries on Super Tuesday, March 8, 1988, when thirteen Southern states would vote on the same day. He didn't anticipate Jesse Jackson's popularity, who won six states in the Super Tuesday voting, plus South Carolina. Gore tied with seven. In April 1988, in a debate in New York City, Gore's comments about Israel and his attacks on Jesse Jackson and Michael Dukakis were viewed negatively. He received only 10% of the vote in the New York primary. Shortly thereafter, he dropped out of the race.

Al called. I was out of the house and he spoke with Ron. I called him back. We both wanted to talk about the election.

"Perhaps we can get together to talk?" I said.

"Soon," he said. "It must be soon."

But it was Friday, and he and I were both leaving over the weekend for a week away.

The next night, in my motel room in Rocky Mount, N.C., I asked for information about Al. A dream answered my request. It was the first about Al in several months.

Information has appeared in the newspapers about Al's decision to withdraw and about ideas he has for the future. I visit Peter, who asks if I have seen the proposals. I say no and feel guilty that I haven't.

Peter draws for me a picture of a geologic formation which is a point of land that forms a triangle into the sea. Behind the triangle is a line of mountains, a low, rocky formation. Al has said that if you draw certain lines and intersect them in the water, than draw a line over the point to the center of the land, you would find "it." I don't know what "it" is, but it is the answer or the treasure, something very significant.

I go to the point in the water, and then to the point on the land mass, where Al appears and we talk. He is wearing a long gray coat, similar to the one I have with me on this trip—clearly, this dream figure is a part of me. The feeling is positive, deep, complex, and rich. We are talking about what the answer is, and what is in the water. We leave the point of land and walk down the left shore onto a boardwalk, then we separate, and I go back to the point. I see John Fortin. I realize that he and Al seem to be the same person, and I embrace him.

When I awoke, I realized that Al and I both felt we had failed—he in his presidential run, and I as co-director of SANE-Freeze—although I had not previously admitted the feeling of failure to myself. I also saw that Al was representing my animus again. He and John Fortin seemed to be two aspects of the animus. Both were parts of me, and in the dream I embraced them.

There was more to the dream:

I go to the point of land and stand on a rock wall. It is like a castle wall with indentations across the top. I hold onto the wall and look down into the water. Below me is a shiny white fish. I want to be with the fish. I try to decide whether to jump into the water, but the water is so far down.

I know that the "Al" part of me is looking for me. I look behind me and see a black man walking out of a cave. He says, "I'll be glad to help you so you don't have to jump." He looks like a man I work with who is warm and gentle, but whom I can't trust to do what he says he is going to do.

"No!" I say. "Don't come close to me! I want to jump!"

He keeps coming, with a kind expression on his face. I keep yelling at him to go back and leave me alone.

I realize that the Point is a druidic tower: the Black Tower. It's an image from the novel, <u>The Mists of Avalon</u>. I scale the wall of the tower. The whole area—land and water—is dark and mysterious. I get onto a very tall ladder that leans against the tower and goes down into the water. It starts to sway, and it only has rungs at the top.

The black man says, "Wait! I'll help you." I say, "No! Go away! I want to do this myself."

What I understood was this: The white fish (Spirit, the light of the unconscious) was calling me. The black man—the unconscious masculine inside me—wished to support my effort to get into the water, the unconscious. The dream seemed to be about wanting to unite with Spirit, and of integrating the various aspects of the animus. There was fear about what resided in my unconscious.

Finally, a month after his withdrawal from the race, Al and I talked. He was in pain about having to withdraw, and our conversation was brief. I was grateful he had called me and felt a kinship with him in his pain. I was still recovering from the SANE-Freeze attempts to discredit me.

Still, my new work was enlivening. Under my leadership, the U.S. Comprehensive Test Ban (CTB) Coalition began to take root. In meetings with the parliamentarians and physicians, other national organizations joined our ranks. During the three years leading up to the January 1991 conference at the United Nations, seventy-five national organizations would become members of the coalition, including religious and faith-based groups, women's groups, disarmament organizations, arms control institutes and research groups, campus groups, Gray Panthers, Jobs for Peace, the American Medical Association, the American Public Health Association, YWCA, and organizations of lawyers, psychologists, economists, radiation victims, veterans, and rural Americans.

As the coalition grew, we coordinated and communicated the breadth of its work back to its members, the media, Congress, and grassroots groups in cities across America. Its goals were to stop all nuclear weapons testing worldwide, to bring about a global CTB treaty, and to help build an infrastructure that would redefine global security. These were important and lofty goals, and I was happy to be a part of this effort. It fueled my passion and fed my soul.

As executive director, my task was to invite the broadest possible participation while holding in mind all of the work that was being done in Washington, around the country, and internationally. I supervised staff, raised funds, coordinated a national strategy and work plan, coordinated media appearances, and worked with members of Congress on legislation.

The CTB coalition and its members engaged in hundreds of activities, including preparing publications targeted for the media, local and national elected officials, organizations, activists, and technical experts. As well, they created and promoted radio and TV spots, television interviews, signature ads, billboards, op-eds, and celebrity speak-outs. U.S. and Soviet scientists jointly published a study on the feasibility of a CTB.

Meanwhile, elected officials and community leaders organized an open letter to President Bush, President Gorbachev, and Prime Minister Thatcher, and worked to pass CTB resolutions at local and state levels, joining 223 already passed. Broad-based coalitions in hundreds of local communities supported this work. U.S. and Soviet mayors held joint meetings in which they issued a call for a test ban and an end to the nuclear arms race.

There was more: A ten-state western tour by U.S. and Soviet radiation victims of nuclear testing; a speaking tour to ten U.S. cities by poet Olzhas Suliemenov, leader of the Soviet anti-testing movement; an International Citizens Congress for a CTB in Kazakhstan; events at the Partial Test Ban Treaty review conferences in Geneva; telegrams to U.N. Ambassador Thomas Pickering; and letters to Barbara Bush, wife of the U.S. President.

Perhaps most courageous were the thousands of U.S. and Canadian citizens who routinely committed civil disobedience at the Nevada Test Site; at Department of Energy facilities in D.C., Nevada, California, and Texas; and at nuclear power plants and weapons facilities elsewhere.

I visited the Nuclear Test Site in 1989, where over 700 underground nuclear explosions have desecrated a land mass the size of Rhode Island, leaving huge craters throughout the Nevada desert. Although the U.S. Department of Energy maintained that it was safe to visit and work at the site, yellow-and-black signs warning "Danger, Nuclear Contamination" were posted throughout the testing grounds. Everyone was required to wear dosimeters to measure their exposure to radiation.

During the 1980s and early 1990s, thousands of people visited the site each year to pay homage to the Shoshone land that the government destroyed but never paid for, and to pray that testing would stop. The Nevada Test Site, like all other nuclear test sites worldwide, is located on land that was once the homeland of people of color. Nuclear test explosions, both underground and in the atmosphere, have brought devastating health consequences to those living downwind of the sites. In the U.S., those most affected were the Shoshone and Paiute tribes, and residents of St. George, Utah.

I traveled to the test site again in 1990 to speak at a rally and support over 1,000 people who had come to commit civil disobedience by walking onto the testing grounds. The event was upbeat, calm, and orderly. Each person crawled under the barbed wire fence and began walking in the direction of the testing facilities, which were beyond our range of sight. Security guards and police moved unhurriedly, grasped the arm of each demonstrator, bound their hands together with a plastic tie, then led them to a large pen, from which they were loaded onto buses and taken to Beatty, Nevada, forty-five miles away and ninety miles north of Las Vegas. In Beatty, each person wrote their name in a ledger before they were freed. Then they had to find a way back to the test site grounds, where cars and vans would take us all back to Las Vegas.

I held onto personal belongings and waited at a permanent encampment located across the road from the test site for their return. I had thought hard about whether to join them in committing civil disobedience. All of us were uncertain how being arrested would be used against us. In the end, I decided it was important that I be able to continue to lead the test ban coalition. Instead of putting myself on the line for one incident, I would put myself on the line for the long-term.

It was a simple but powerful exercise for those who participated and for those who watched. Each year thousands of Americans and Canadians were willing to travel across country to Nevada and be arrested in order to protest the nuclear arms race.

The test ban coalition was working with Congress to pass a moratorium on nuclear testing when, in October 1989, a popular movement began in the central Asian republic of Kazakhstan to close down the Soviet test site at Semipalatinsk.

Kazakh poet and public figure Olzhas Suliemenov, scheduled to read his poetry on television, instead announced a public gathering in the capital city of Alma-Ata to inform the Kazakhs about the effects of nuclear testing on the Kazakh people. Word reached us that 5,000 Kazakhs tried to crowd into his office to call for an end to Soviet testing. The meeting launched the "Nevada-Semipalatinsk Movement," named for the U.S. and Soviet test sites.

As impossible as it seemed in the days before the Internet, in less than a week two million people signed a petition asking Gorbachev to stop nuclear testing. Three days later Suliemenov hand carried the petitions to Gorbachev and the Supreme Soviet. A Soviet moratorium on testing was declared, effective immediately, thus providing the impetus for U.S. activists to intensify their efforts.

CTB coalition members were thrilled. We knew the U.S. government would not stop testing unless the U.S.S.R. stopped first. We were also aware of this irony: our democratic government had said repeatedly that the Soviet people did not have a voice in the political life of their country, all the while our government was not listening to us.

Closing the test site was a great victory for the Kazakh people, who had not been told about the effects of the nuclear tests, nor why such a high percentage of their people, animals, and crops were diseased, disfigured, and dying. Hundreds of thousands of Kazakhs lived and farmed within fifty miles of the test site, where radioactive emissions were routinely vented into the atmosphere. Sheep, horses, and goats drank from enormous pools formed by nuclear craters. Once the Kazakhs understood that their government had not only not protected them, but had knowingly exposed them to devastating health consequences, Kazakh leaders began to prepare for an international conference that would call for an end to testing worldwide: the International Citizens Congress for a Nuclear Test Ban.

In May 1990, I traveled to the U.S.S.R. to attend the congress. Six hundred delegates from twenty countries met in Moscow, then flew to Alma-Ata, the capital of Kazakhstan, not far from the Mongolian steppes.

Alma-Ata is situated at the base of the Tien-Shan Mountains, where snow glimmers on peaks that tower above the city. We arrived late at night and rose early to children singing and handing flowers and other gifts to the participants. The congress was a whirlwind of speeches, banquets, and a bus tour to a large athletic complex in the mountains. We heard a litany of what the Soviet, U.S., British, French, and Chinese governments had done to their own people in the name of national security. Physicians, scientists, and people living downwind of the test sites told of health and environmental consequences of radiation poisoning: birth defects, stillbirths, cancer, diabetes, infertility, insanity, suicide.

Over and over, in hushed tones, speakers named the test sites: Novaya Zemlya; Semipalatinsk; Mercury, Nevada; the Marshall Islands; and China's Lop Nor. (Over the years, nuclear bombs were also exploded in New Mexico, Colorado, Mississippi, Alaska, six additional atolls and islands of the Pacific, Australia, Algeria, the Ukraine, Turkmenistan, Uzbekistan, India, Pakistan, South Africa, Japan, North Korea, and several other sites in Nevada and Kazakhstan.)

During atmospheric testing in the 1950s and 1960s, the U.S. government did not tell the American people about the dangers of radiation exposure. They did not evacuate nearby cities, towns, or Native American reservations. Soldiers were stationed in trenches to observe the explosions. When they covered their eyes with their arms to avoid looking directly at the blast, radiation illuminated the bones in their arms.

Atmospheric testing lasted from 1951-58; underground testing had been conducted since 1961. The figures are astonishing: Worldwide atmospheric testing produced a total yield of 438 megatons, the equivalent of 29,200 Hiroshimas, as though a Hiroshima bomb had exploded in the atmosphere every eleven hours from 1951 to 1987. Once every eleven hours for thirty-six years.

A Department of Energy (DOE) map published in the late 1980s shows the spread of radioactive material throughout the United States caused by atmospheric testing. Vast areas of plutonium and uranium contamination extend through every state in the continental U.S., predicted to remain radioactive indefinitely. Added to this is the devastation to agricultural land, livestock, water sources, and human life around nuclear production plants at Hanford, Washington; Savannah, Georgia; Rocky Flats, Colorado; Portsmouth and Fernald, Ohio—the extent of the damage still unrevealed by the U.S. government.

This and similar information about the other nuclear countries filled our days at the congress. On the last day, participants joined 10,000 Alma-Atans in a march down the main thoroughfare asking for a permanent closing of the Soviet test site. The marchers carried twenty-foot-long banners to which were pinned watercolor paintings by Kazakh secondary students depicting their concerns about the nuclear arms race. The paintings were well-executed and thoughtful. One was of a tree with a line down the center. On one side grass and flowers shimmered in the sun; on the other, all had been devastated by a nuclear bomb.

Following a rally in the sports stadium, we said goodbye to our hosts and boarded a flight to Semipalatinsk (Semey), 550 miles north of Alma-Ata, a former junction of caravan trails. Before the Russian Revolution, more than 11,000 camels passed through Semey annually, crossing the vast desert that sprawls to the west and south, an area rarely experienced by Western travelers. Once in Semey, we would take buses into the desert to the village of Karaul, thirty miles downwind of the Soviet test site, meet with villagers, and return to Semey that night.

The sun glinted off the wings of the Aeroflot plane as we nosed down at the provincial capital. Several hundred people bearing gifts thronged to greet us, including a dozen young women in white dresses and embroidered velvet vests carrying trays of bread and salt, the traditional Kazakh welcome. Above the hubbub rose the tinkling of flutes. Lining the passageway from the plane to the street were vendors selling postcards, pins, and other souvenirs. I stopped to buy a stuffed camel with Oriental carpet saddlebags—a Kazakh to take home— then boarded one of thirteen red-and-white buses for the trip to Karaul.

Our caravan rode over dry, rocky desert similar to the area surrounding the Nevada Test Site, mostly boulders, scrub, and a few low hills. The terrain was broken uplands, bare and eroded. During the first two hours, we passed fewer than a dozen houses and saw no one. At 1:30 p.m. word passed among us that we would be stopping for lunch, which was confusing news as there appeared to be nowhere to eat. Suddenly the lead bus drove off the road and onto an open field.

As our bus joined the others parked in a long line, we saw across the field a flat-roofed corrugated building the size of a large warehouse, with doors flung open in our direction. Near where the buses parked were half a dozen portable toilets interspersed with portable sinks. Strung behind the sinks was a clothesline upon which mint green hand towels fluttered in the wind.

"Lunch is this way!" someone yelled, motioning toward the shed. Halfway across the rock-strewn field we came upon a band of musicians nestled into the hillside playing Kazakh music as women in brightly colored dresses danced.

My mind tried to make sense of this. Where had the shed, the dancers and musicians, the toilets and sinks, come from? Who had arranged this? Stepping inside the shed, I gasped.

Costumed waitresses in white blouses, embroidered skirts and vests, directed us to banquet tables fifty feet long, set with white linen cloths. On the tables were red roses in crystal vases, platters of breads and sweets, and bottles of wine. Hung over the back of each chair was a tea towel embroidered with cherries, a gift for each of us to take home. Steaming bowls of meats, vegetables, noodles, wines, sweets, and fancy liqueurs were plied on us for the next hour, while we murmured and exclaimed over the generosity and graciousness of our hosts.

One of the first to reboard the bus, I sat down next to Ted, a former U.S. nuclear bomb designer whose job had been to draw circles around Soviet cities on a map in order to determine how many people would be killed by what size bomb. He had become a test ban advocate in recent years, a spokesman about the danger of nuclear addiction, how the explosive power of the bombs could run in a scientist's blood.

"Can you believe this?" He gestured toward the shed as tears welled in his eyes. "We would never do anything like this for Soviets visiting our test site."

"I know. It's hard to take it all in."

Ted shook his head. "It's so far beyond anything I could have conceived, being treated like this. I don't know what to think."

I took Ted's hand and we sat for a few moments in silence before others boarded the bus.

An hour later we passed through Karaul, lonesome village of the Kazakh steppes. The buses crept slowly as we neared the village. Hovels leaned against one another, each indistinguishable from the next, all the color of dirt. One lone dog limped down the lane, moving away from us as though it did not want us to see its pathetic state. The place was caked with dust and smelled of dust.

The buses rounded a knoll and pulled into an open field near a barbed-wire fence, where a sign indicated the perimeter of the Soviet nuclear test site. Inside a padlocked gate, a dirt road wound across the field and disappeared over a dune to the testing grounds, thirty kilometers away.

We exited the buses to a warm, dry, desert wind; the

earth beneath our feet was rocky, rugged. I bent and touched the earth, felt the lumps of rock in my hand, the dust sifting through my fingers. I moistened a finger and held it up; the wind was slight, almost unmoving.

To our right was the knoll, twenty feet high, gently sloping, and at its base, a gathering of perhaps 200 villagers from Karaul. A banner ten feet long swayed on poles, proclaiming "No More Nuclear Tests" in English, Russian, and French. A microphone and sound system had been set up near the knoll, and a semicircle of fifty yurts spread out to our left, at the far end of which stood a stage with a corrugated roof, where half a dozen young men and women played flutes and three-stringed *dombras*, an instrument of the Kazakh steppes.

Near the knoll, the Kazakhs stood in families: a mother and two children here; a couple with their grown son; four older men, grizzled, their faces plaintive, their eyes darting to catch mine. Everyone wore tattered dark-colored clothes, their hands and faces dark and leathery from the sun. They did not reach out their hands to us, but they seemed to want to know us with their eyes.

We guests walked among the villagers, and with the help of interpreters, engaged in conversation with village families. Some of us knew a few words of Russian; I also carried a small dictionary. If they understood my meager attempts, they nodded and sometimes their faces lit up. I felt that each word we both understood was a gift.

Youths, their eyes eager to meet ours, proffered torn scraps of paper no larger than a butterfly's wing and asked for our autographs; most lacked a pen. Mothers and fathers held up their children to show us the harelips, bulging foreheads, missing arms, and short, stubby, twisted legs. Some of these children were adults. At the congress we had heard stories about the health devastation of large populations of Kazakhstan caused by nuclear testing, but the stories hardly prepared us for what we were seeing. I felt like weeping. I wanted to get down on my knees and weep onto the Earth. What could I do but look into their eyes and wish them well in whatever words I had?

The rally had begun, with speakers from Germany, France,

Britain, Kazakhstan, Russia, and the U.S. Interspersed among the speeches, villagers told stories of family members dying of cancer and diabetes, of children with birth defects, and of young men, discovering they were infertile, taking their own lives. I found it almost impossible to listen to the speeches, wishing to spend my time at the outer edges of the crowd, among the families that seemed as moved by this event as I was. Finally I drifted away from the center of the crowd and stood further back, among the men and women of Karaul.

After the rally we crossed the field to the semicircle of yurts. In the center, men and women in embroidered garments demonstrated sheep shearing, quilt making, and traditional embroidery. On the stage a group was enacting a play about ending nuclear testing, followed by more songs and dances. I tried to be present for these events, but my heart was heavy with what I had just experienced.

After dark a bell rang for dinner. Each of us went to the yurt that corresponded to the number we had received on our bus. Entering the flap of yurt #46, I found myself inside a wood-framed felt dome with floor and walls lined with Oriental carpets called *tekemets.* A set of low tables formed a crescent, with cushions on the outside and the center open for serving food and drink. My twenty dinner companions and I sat on the cushions and introduced ourselves: Germans, Kazakhs, Russians, Japanese, and Americans. A Kazakh man in white shirt, embroidered vest, and pants gathered at the ankles poured wine, and we raised our glasses to world peace.

Dinner was a dozen courses of meat, bread, vegetables, wine, and desserts, throughout which we toasted to world peace and sang songs in our many languages. At midnight word passed through the yurts that it was time to re-board the buses. Someone suggested the Soviet children's peace song and taught it to those who had never sung it. We placed our hands on each other's shoulders and, swaying, sang together:

May there always be sunshine,
May there always be blue skies,
May there always be mama,
May there always be me.

The Silence that Kills.

Between 1983 and 1994, over 40,000 people were arrested in the U.S. and Canada for committing nonviolent civil disobedience while protesting the nuclear arms race and nuclear industry. Civil disobedience took place at dozens of research installations, storage areas, missile silos, test sites, military bases, corporate and government offices, and nuclear power plants.

Year after year, people traveled thousands of miles to the Nuclear Test Site (NTS) in the Nevada desert to protest nuclear weapons development and nuclear test explosions. Protesters included scientists, physicians, teachers, retirees, businessmen and women, and Hollywood actors. They included Caucasians, African Americans, Native Americans, Hispanics, and other races. In all, over 14,600 people were arrested at the NTS.

The *Los Angeles Times* was the only U.S. newspaper to consistently cover civil disobedience at the test site. The vast majority of the media refused to cover the story. Corporate owners of the mainstream media and weapons manufacturers kept our actions from being made public. If nuclear testing and the nuclear arms race were halted, it would threaten their financial holdings. They were willing to jeopardize the health and well-being of the American people and people worldwide in order to increase their profits.

Bolstered with knowledge about the vast numbers of people willing to be arrested for our cause, others would have supported our efforts with their presence, donations, and prayers. A larger and better funded movement could have brought an even quicker end to nuclear testing and possibly a greater drawdown of U.S. and Soviet nuclear forces. Equally important, it would have given a voice back to the people that is rightfully theirs in a democratic society.

Nuclear Resistance Arrests, U.S. and Canada, 1982-1994
(Compiled by the *Nuclear Resister*, Tucson, Arizona, 1994)

Year	# of arrests	# arrests NTS	# of total sites	# of actions
1994	910	240	41	73
1993	1,000	230	37	80
1992	2,480	1,700+	40	90
1991	2,550	2,105	32	65
1990	3,000	1,731	41	85
1989	5,530	2,314	75	150
1988	4,470	2,800	65	160
1987	5,300	2,500+	70	180
1986	3,200	640	75	165
1985	3,500	254		170
1984	3,010	76		60
1983	5,300	10		40
Totals:	40,250	14,600		1,318

15
The Nations Gather

In the years 1957 to 1963, following reports of strontium 90 found in mothers' milk, respectable, middle-aged women wearing white gloves and flowered hats picketed the White House and called on the Kremlin to save their children and their planet from the radiation effects of nuclear testing in the atmosphere.

At one such event, held on November 1, 1961, at the height of the Cold War, 50,000 women marched in sixty U.S. cities to demonstrate against nuclear weapons. President John F. Kennedy watched from the White House as 1,500 women gathered at the foot of the Washington Monument.

Two years later, President Kennedy and Premier Nikita Khrushchev signed the Partial Test Ban Treaty (PTBT), prohibiting nuclear testing in the atmosphere, in outer space, and under water. Widespread concern about the radioactive fallout of atmospheric tests was a major impetus for the treaty. The Soviet Union wanted to ban testing underground as well, but when the U.S. insisted that verification include visits to each other's test sites, the Soviets refused. Although it fell short of its goal, the preamble to the PTBT affirms the aim of discontinuing "all test explosions of nuclear weapons for all time."

Unlike other arms control treaties, the PTBT also contained a provision that allowed the treaty to be amended easily at a future date. A simple majority of the 118 parties was required, but that majority had to include the United States, Great Britain, and the Soviet Union—the Original Parties. Most countries eventually signed and ratified the treaty, but China, France, and North Korea, known to have tested nuclear weapons, did not sign, largely because the treaty excluded them from being Original Parties.

For twenty-five years, U.S.-U.S.S.R. negotiations for a comprehensive test ban were deadlocked, with the Soviets pressing for a CTB, and the U.S. and her ally Great Britain refusing to support a test ban so that they could develop new nuclear weapons. Parliamentarians for Global Action saw the amendment process as a powerful way to force the U.S. into a CTB and thus began to work for a conference to amend the treaty.

All the nuclear weapons "threshold" states—India, Pakistan, Libya, Iran, Iraq, South Africa, Israel, Argentina, and Brazil—were parties to the PTBT, so an amendment to the treaty would bind them all to a halt in testing. It would be a brilliant step toward solving the problem of the spread of nuclear weapons.

After years of hard work, on August 5, 1988, the 25th anniversary of the treaty, the ambassadors of five non-nuclear-weapon countries—Indonesia, Mexico, Peru, Sri Lanka, and Yugoslavia—visited the ambassadors of the Original Parties to submit an amendment to transform the treaty into a comprehensive test ban. The process required that one-third of the parties formally request the conference. Six months later, forty parties were on board, and the Original Parties were legally bound to convene the conference.

A date was set for January 1991. A vote on the amendment itself was unlikely, given the position of the U.S. and U.K., but a vote could be taken on whether to continue the process.

In the fall of 1990, leading up to the conference, a delegation of members of the Supreme Soviet, the House of Commons, and the U.S. Congress requested meetings with Mikhail Gorbachev, Margaret Thatcher, and President Bush. Meanwhile

Kazakh poet-activist Olzhas Suliemenov toured ten U.S. cities, beginning with a rally at the White House. The tour included university speeches, Hollywood fundraisers, and visits to St. George, Utah, and the Paiute Nation, both downwind of the Nevada test site. Two weeks later, an international conference was held in Las Vegas, followed by a mass action at the test site.

On January 6, 1991, the treaty conference convened with 100 of the 118 parties to the treaty participating. Test ban supporters planned numerous activities to occur that week in New York City, including a convocation, evening vigils, and a street action and rally. U.S. and Soviet mayors also met in New York that week to press for a comprehensive test ban.

My role was to organize a lobbying day for those who had traveled from around the world to observe the conference. I conducted a training session for one hundred citizen lobbyists, whose task would be to request a meeting with their delegate and express the hopes of the people of their country that the parties would negotiate a CTB. The meetings were to be cordial, with citizens telling why they had traveled to New York and why they cared about a test ban. For the next two days small groups could be seen meeting with their delegates in the public areas of the United Nations. The U.S. delegate, Mary E. Hoinkes, refused a meeting. However, the lobby day was declared a great success. It was the first time groups of citizens had lobbied their delegates at the United Nations.

The citizen lobbyists were subsequently invited to address the delegates in a special session, and thirty of us signed up. We would each have three minutes to make our remarks. For the session, we sat in theater-style seats to the left of the delegates, looking out over the conference. The room was full except for Ms. Hoinkes, whose absence was obvious to everyone.

Speakers described the devastating effects of nuclear testing on the health and well-being of the people living near test sites and the destruction of fishing grounds in the Pacific Ocean. I was tenth on the program. As I awaited my turn, I thought about the discourtesy shown by Ms. Hoinkes' absence. At the podium I talked about the support for a test ban by 80%

of the American people and the wide range of activities and involvement of people at all levels of society. I concluded by noting the absence of the U.S. delegate and announced that I would call her to request a special meeting where she could hear the concerns of the fifty U.S. citizens who had traveled from many parts of the country.

When the session was finished, I phoned Ms. Hoinkes in her hotel room to tell her that we missed her at the meeting and that the U.S. attendees wanted to meet with her. She was reluctant, but agreed to meet with two U.S. attendees. I insisted that all fifty be allowed to attend. She said no, not fifty, and suggested an upstairs lounge. I knew that all fifty would be there.

When we arrived, Ms. Hoinkes was seated in an open area of the lounge with three chairs nearby. All fifty attendees entered the area and sat down on the floor close to her. She was clearly dismayed that everyone had come. We thanked her for agreeing to the meeting. I asked those wishing to speak to share their concerns. The speakers identified themselves and told stories of the effects of nuclear testing on their families and communities:

"I live in St. George, Utah, downwind of the Nevada Test Site, where the incidence of cancer and diabetes is very high. My daughter died of leukemia at the age of four."

"I am a Paiute. My home is the Shivwits Reservation, downwind of the test site. Everyone on the reservation has diabetes and skin diseases."

"I'm a grandmother and I've watched several members of my family die of cancer."

"When I was a child, I saw a nuclear test explosion in the atmosphere. Several women in my family have died of breast cancer."

Ms. Hoinkes listened and said little. When we were done, she thanked us for our comments. The meeting was over, and we left. She had not explained why she was absent from the speeches, nor had she apologized.

In the final session, the parties to the treaty voted on whether to reconvene the conference at a future date. The vote was 74 for, 2 against, and 19 abstaining. Only the U.S. and Great Britain voted against the resolution, stating that a treaty conference was not the appropriate forum for negotiating a test ban—although, as we had seen for decades, they had stonewalled the test ban talks in Geneva.

The treaty delegates and the citizen delegates knew that the conference had raised the issue to the international level, involving over 100 countries and drawing the attention of the U.S. Congress. The CTB campaign was ready to refocus its efforts on Washington.

The Few and the Many.

The United States of America was founded on the principle that all people are created equal and guaranteed certain "unalienable" rights. Those rights include the right to assemble, the right to free speech, and the right to be represented by an elected official. I and millions of other American children were taught that our democracy was the best system on Earth. As adults, I and millions of others have discovered that the system contains a fatal flaw: it allows those with large sums of money to influence politics to their own end.

When kings and queens and presidents and members of Congress, who claim power through their position or their office, do not provide for those under their care, it is up to the many to do what is necessary so that all might lead decent lives. When the few are concerned solely about their own needs, then the many must rise up on behalf of everyone.

This may mean putting one's self in harm's way. When Gandhi and his seventy-eight "activists of truth and resolution" marched to the Indian coast in March 1930 to pick up clumps of salt in defiance of British law, they put their lives at risk. Tens of thousands joined the march to the sea and broke the law by picking up salt. Within a month, over 60,000 had been arrested. On May 21, at the Dharasana Salt Works in Gujarat, British police, using metal-tipped clubs, viciously beat 2,500 men who marched to the salt pen and attempted to remove the barbed wire. The activists' courage and willingness to sacrifice inspired millions of other Indians and gained the support of many outsiders. It was a major force in India's gaining independence from Britain.

In Montgomery, Alabama, on December 1, 1955, Rosa Parks refused the bus driver's order that she give up her seat for a white passenger. Her action was not the first of its kind, as at least five other women had taken similar stands in previous years. But Parks was known throughout Montgomery's African-American community. Her civil disobedience sparked the thirteen-month Montgomery bus boycott that led to the Supreme Court declaring segregation on public buses unconstitutional. It was a milestone in the civil rights movement. The success of the boycott was attributed to Parks' willingness to commit civil disobedience, the leadership of Martin Luther King, Jr., and others, and "the nameless cooks and maids who walked endless miles for a year to bring about the breach in the walls of segregation." (Mary Fair Burks, Women's Political Council, Montgomery, Alabama)

Why should one take such a risk for the sake of the many? I believe that those who stand up for the rights of others increase the flow of divine grace to themselves, and those who do not stand up, stop the flow of that same divine grace.

When one stops the flow of love to others, one closes the door to love. Darkness creeps in. One stops the flow to one's self.

16
In Time

What had been the nascent fruits of our labor were growing with each passing day. In 1991, those who had worked for more than a decade to end nuclear testing sensed the possibility of a future harvest. A U.S. moratorium on testing seemed within reach.

Activists continued their work with dedication and fervor. Church bells tolled in Cleveland, Ohio, and other cities each time there was a nuclear test anywhere in the world. Farmers who lived near an air force base in Wyoming created an enormous peace symbol in the fields to remind pilots on takeoff that peace was the goal. Media interviews, newspaper ads, letters to the editor, and speak-outs at district congressional meetings took place in hundreds of towns and cities throughout the U.S. With a Soviet moratorium in place and the Amendment Conference behind us, the U.S. CTB Coalition focused on getting a moratorium passed by Congress.

As the campaign intensified its legislative work, I received a phone call from a California filmmaker named David Brown. David was calling with a request: Ram Dass, the spiritual teacher who had first touched my life in the early 1970s, was coming to Washington to conduct interviews for a PBS television series he was producing called "Reaching Out." One of the interviewees, a member of Congress, had cancelled. Would it be possible for Ram Dass to interview me about compassion and social change? Yes, I said. Of course.

I first saw Ram Dass in the days when he sported long

hair, beads, and a beard on a videotape being shown on a small black-and-white TV in Topanga Canyon in 1970. Soon thereafter he came to Los Angeles to address a standing-room-only crowd at the Shrine Auditorium. I was so taken by his message that my friends and I stayed until 2:00 a.m., among the very last to leave. He became instantly famous in 1971 for his book, *Be Here Now*, which eventually sold over ten million copies worldwide. Years later I heard him speak in Nashville, and in the intervening years read his books and listened to audiotapes of his talks dozens of times.

It would be a thrill to meet him. More, I was delighted that he wanted to interview me.

We met in a house in the D.C. suburbs where Ram Dass and his cameraman had set up for the interviews. He welcomed me warmly and explained how things would go. We would talk on videotape for about an hour, from which he would draw excerpts to show to an audience of about 1,000 in Oakland, California. The audience would be a part of the PBS program as well.

As the camera rolled, Ram Dass asked me about my work, what motivated me, and how I brought my spiritual values into the work. I told the story of how Spirit had struck me with lightning, nudging me to write a letter to a congressman for a neighboring district. From that startling beginning, I told him, I had become the director of the CTB Coalition. He was delighted by my story, especially of how Spirit had led me to act in the political arena from a place of love. Ram Dass told me that before my interview he had thought of compassion as being a heart response to a person or persons in need; for example, to those who were homeless or beggars on the street. He had not thought of compassion as motivation for the kind of work I did.

He decided to use the following excerpt for the program:

Caroline: "We will either destroy ourselves, or we will go forward and be able to transform into a partnership society and a partnership world where we work cooperatively. And that's where I think we are. I think we are very close to the fork in the road."

Ram Dass: "You don't think we're beyond the fork?"

Caroline: "I don't think we're beyond the fork."

Ram Dass: "You think there's still choice. There's still space."

Caroline: "Yes, I do. What do you think?"

Ram Dass: "I don't know. I really don't know. People have to leap out into the unknown. And I notice that somehow we have gotten so obsessed with security that we don't leap. We just build our little walls and protect. And I think that is doomed. And I don't know what that turning point is. That's the mystery."

Caroline: "I agree with you that the way we are doing things is doomed, for sure."

He was asking me if we had time to save the planet and its inhabitants from the collision course we were on. I felt certain that it was not too late.

In mid-1991, Representative Mike Kopetski of Oregon, a new member of Congress elected with support from peace organizations, agreed to put his name at the top of a piece of legislation for a nuclear testing moratorium. Kopetski saw this as an opportunity to work on a major issue where he could make a difference.

Washington's community of arms control lobbyists decided to make CTB legislation a priority. A network of national organizations pulled together, meeting regularly and working with grassroots groups to develop co-sponsors in the House. Over the course of nine months, the testing issue rose to an even higher priority as it appeared that a sufficient number of representatives would sign onto the bill, thus ensuring a successful floor vote. Once there were enough co-sponsors, the bill would be voted on by House Defense and Appropriations

Committees, then move to the House floor. The bill would follow a similar path in the Senate.

Before any votes could be taken, we needed co-sponsors in the Senate. We proposed a date in early 1992 for activists to come to Washington to lobby key senators. We selected nine senators and invited activists from those states to participate. As a result of the lobby day, seven senators signed onto the legislation, the beginning of a cohort of sponsors in the Senate.

One by one, additional senators signed onto the bill. Momentum continued to grow until at the end of April 1992 there were thirty-two. It was not nearly enough: A minimum of fifty-one co-sponsors would be needed to pass the bill on the Senate floor. National lobbyists and their grassroots networks continued to lobby individual senators, thrilled when Ohio Senator John Glenn signed on, who had not previously supported the test ban. During May and early June, Senate co-sponsorship increased from thirty-two to fifty.

Gore was not among the fifty. Legislative strategists decided that Gore's support was pivotal, as his decision to sign onto the legislation would bring other senators with him. Over the course of two weeks, national arms control and disarmament organizations sent a parade of lobbyists to talk to Aaron Wolfe, who wouldn't budge. He and Gore contended that nuclear testing was essential if the U.S. was to maintain a reliable "stable" of nuclear weapons.

Gore was in Rio de Janeiro for the environmental summit, June 3-14, but gaining Senate co-sponsors was an urgent matter. The work had to go forward, which was why lobbyists were pressing Aaron.

I considered what I knew about Gore and Wolfe's position and decided that I had an idea that might persuade Aaron. I called and told him I had a proposal to discuss with him. How soon could we talk? He had a full schedule but wanted to hear what I had to say. Could I stop by the following afternoon?

Aaron met me in the reception area of Gore's Senate office. He had fifteen minutes between meetings. We sat in a corner with the arms of our chairs almost touching, where we could talk away from the flow of traffic, without others overhearing.

"I know that lobbyists have approached you about the test ban legislation."

Aaron nodded somberly, eyes on the floor. It was Aaron's way of listening deeply and considering what I was saying.

"I also understand that you have not found their arguments convincing. I want to propose a different way of thinking about this."

He looked up, skeptical perhaps, but clearly interested.

"I believe that you can support a moratorium on testing and also have what you want, and what Gore wants as well."

"Okay, say more." His expression was still somber, but I detected a slight glint in his eyes.

"You say that nuclear weapons do not need to be tested in the ground, that they can be tested by computer. Is this correct?"

"Yes, that's true. We have that technology."

"So one doesn't need to continue testing underground. Is that correct?"

"Yes, it is." He waited for more.

"The time is right for this, Aaron. The Soviets have taken the first step. If the U.S. doesn't respond with a moratorium, the Soviets will start testing again, leading to further escalation of an arms race that is already way out of control.

"By signing onto the test ban legislation, Gore becomes a good guy in the eyes of the American people and people around the world, without giving up what concerns him, which is the ability to continue to keep the arsenal viable."

He nodded, looked at me. "You've made some good points. It's possible. I'll have to give it more thought."

"Okay. I appreciate that." I collected my briefcase. "When does Al return from Rio?"

"Next Friday."

I smiled, standing. "All the best to your family."

He stood and hugged me. "Thanks. I'll let you know how this goes."

I didn't hear from Aaron before Gore returned. Whether there had been a shift in Aaron's thinking, I did not know.

On Friday, just back from Rio, Senator Al Gore, Jr., walked onto the Senate floor to make a speech to his colleagues. In the speech he signed onto the Senate legislation for a moratorium on nuclear tests. Seven other senators followed suit, persuaded by Gore's stance. Aaron had written the speech.

Lasting Change.

Harvey Jackins, the leader of the Re-evaluation Counseling communities until his death in 1999, told co-counselors that one cannot make lasting change without building relationships. He told us never to step back from the contacts we make, always to build on these, to grow a larger and larger network of contacts and friends.

In 1987, counseling me in front of an RC leaders' workshop on "Discharging Fear of Nuclear Weapons," Harvey had spurred me personally to take on the challenge of ending the nuclear arms race. By this, he meant for me to take this as my goal, to agree to do it single-handedly if necessary. When I said, yes, I would accept that challenge, he looked at me hard and said he didn't believe me. Perhaps he thought my tone of voice was unconvincing, or that I should show more emotion. However calm I appeared, I was quite serious, and others in the forty-person audience said they felt that I was as well.

A few months later I applied for and was hired to be the director of the Nuclear Weapons Freeze Campaign, thus beginning my disarmament work at the national and international level. Whether Harvey was pleased with how far I was able to go, I did not know, as I subsequently dropped out of contact with him, and he later passed away. I only knew that I had gone further than I dreamed possible.

Harvey was as committed to world change as anyone I had ever met. Trusting his guidance, I built deep, lasting relationships with people I initially thought were inaccessible. I made a commitment and held onto that commitment like a rope up a mountain. It was ten years after I initiated the relationships with Gore and Wolfe that the relationships became the ground upon which they could decide to support the comprehensive test ban.

No manipulation was involved, no promise of funds for future election campaigns, no threats of funding Gore's opponents. There was merely, simply, a history of loving them both unconditionally, of getting to know them in a deep and personal way. I knew them well enough to know what it was they wanted and how their support of a test ban would further their goals. Given this history together, Aaron Wolfe knew when he heard my perspective that it could be done. Further, I had given him a motivation to do it: Gore would be seen as a savior.

And there you have it, dear reader. How to make lasting change: Build loving relationships with those in positions of power while holding fast to your goals and ideals.

17
The Glass Elevator

On Sunday night, July 7, 1992, I had a dream. Or, rather, the dream had me.

I am at the Nevada Test Site, where a nuclear bomb is about to be exploded underground. Test site workers put me in a glass elevator suspended over Ground Zero in order for me to feel the power that is to be unleashed by the explosion. As the countdown begins, I am lowered in the elevator to just above ground level. I huddle in a corner of the elevator to prepare myself for the explosion.

The bomb goes off, and the energy that is unleashed is beyond description or comprehension. An explosion of white light transforms the atoms and cells of my physical self into white light as well.

I awoke deeply shaken. A tremendous energy surged through me. I touched my arms, my legs; I was still in one piece. The shaking I felt was profound. What could possibly be the meaning of this dream? The power of this experience was matched only by the lightning bolt that struck my neck in June 1983.

I thought about the dream as I showered, dressed, and ate breakfast. It was Monday morning, and I took the Metro subway into Washington, D.C., for the weekly meeting of lobbyists who were working to end the nuclear arms race. The meetings were held at Blair House, less than 100 yards from the Hart Senate Office Building. The morning was brisk, the air fresh. My head cleared on the short walk from the subway.

As I approached the building, David Culp, a disarmament lobbyist and friend, came out of the building to greet me. I was halfway up the steps when he stopped me. "Have you heard the news?" He was clearly excited.

"No." I shook my head. "What news?" I had not seen the *Washington Post* or turned on the television before heading into the city.

"Clinton has named Gore as his vice president."

I was stunned. I saw that my dream was about Gore's new role. My psyche had registered this news just hours before I heard the announcement. A nuclear explosion was an apt metaphor for how significant I felt his role would be.

Gore's appointment was a surprise to most of us, an exciting and promising prospect for the future of the nation and the world. The Monday lobby group felt this, and many others did as well. Bill Clinton had declared publicly that he would support a halt in nuclear testing if elected president and, with Gore co-sponsoring the legislation in the Senate, it was clear that Gore would support him on the test ban.

Our work was not over, not yet. The route for passage of a testing moratorium through Congress was circuitous, due to the opposition of several congressional leaders. Working with key members of Congress for the next few weeks, we maneuvered the bill through five successful floor votes and numerous committee votes as well. Normally, it took just one vote on the House floor and one on the Senate floor to pass a piece of legislation. As the bill made its way through various votes, then became thwarted, we changed tactics and added the moratorium language to a different bill. During the process, the moratorium was attached to both the Energy and Water Bill and the Defense Bill, in an effort to circumvent members of Congress who opposed its passage. At one point we learned that President Bush would not veto the Energy and Water bill, regardless if it included a testing moratorium, so we focused our efforts in that direction.

Grassroots lobbying in key states and congressional districts was crucial. I raised $9,000 from San Francisco's Ploughshares Foundation, a longtime supporter of the Freeze, to support grassroots activity. My colleagues and I divided a portion of the funds among grassroots groups in eleven congressional districts, where members of Congress were swing votes in the House Appropriations Committee. The funds were used for phone banking, local media, and intensive lobbying. In two weeks we had enough votes to win in the House Appropriations Committee, even though the chair of the committee was against the moratorium.

Some of the funds were also used to air radio spots developed by SANE-Freeze and Physicians for Social Responsibility in Louisiana, Tennessee, and Oregon, states where senators were crucial to the success of the bill. These small efforts, with this small amount of funding, made a huge difference in the bill's success.

The Senate Armed Services Committee would consider the bill as well, which was not a hopeful prospect, as the chair of the committee, Senator Sam Nunn, opposed a test ban. When the leadership of the committee met, however, they did not kill the bill. Instead, they made several changes to the legislation, reducing the proposed twelve-month moratorium to nine months and adding various other stipulations, then voted to send the bill to the Senate floor. This result was due to a mysterious blessing: Sen. Nunn had not shown up for the meeting in time to oppose the moratorium.

In the end, President George Bush, Sr., signed the Energy and Water Bill into law with the moratorium language included. He was unwilling to veto the bill because it contained major funding for a pet project, the Supercollider destined for his home state of Texas. Bush also knew that Clinton was likely to win the election and that Clinton would support a test ban; thus, it was futile to oppose the moratorium. The U.S. conducted its last nuclear test on September 23, 1992.

In November, as the history shows, Bill Clinton and Al Gore, Jr., were elected president and vice president of the United States. Gore and Wolfe became two of President Clinton's top advisors on foreign policy, meeting each morning with the president in the White House. Clinton would extend the test ban moratorium in July 1993, March 1994, and again January 1995, while negotiations for a global test ban treaty continued in Geneva.

Thanks to Clinton, Gore, Wolfe, and other top advisors, the long-awaited Comprehensive Test Ban Treaty was signed by seventy-one nations on September 24, 1996, including the five acknowledged nuclear powers: the United States, Russia, France, the United Kingdom, and the People's Republic of China. The signatories pledged not to conduct any nuclear weapon or other test explosion and to prohibit such explosion on their territory.

I have thought about the glass elevator dream on many occasions. I understood that the explosion was about the changes that Gore would bring in his role as vice president, but I often wondered if there was more.

In summer 2011, I pondered again the images of the glass elevator and the nuclear explosion. These weighed on my awareness as I worked on this book and signed up for a writing retreat in order to renew a focus on writing poetry. Halfway through the retreat, the leader arranged for a van to take participants to an art center in the hills outside of town. The setting was gorgeous; the center overlooked verdant mountains in all directions.

There was only one exhibit: metalwork by the artist Jan Hendrix. I brightened as I approached the front doors, where a ten-foot high, lacey white tree made of metal greeted me. It was a powerful image, evoking the majesty of nature. I wandered through the exhibit slowly, which was spread out through a room half the size of a football field. Some pieces were like small dioramas displayed on tables; others were large enough to walk in and through.

Floating above one table was a metal structure suspended

by plastic threads that looked exactly like the glass elevator of my dream. The work was called "Model of Lament."

The piece was a white rectangular box held together by x-shaped beams. It was supposedly metal and glass, but without any actual glass, like a dollhouse with openings for windows. Inside were two businessmen, standing apart from one another, and underneath the elevator, the figure of a woman with flowing hair and long skirt who carried a briefcase. These three figures were black metal cutouts: flat, shadowy silhouettes. The men appeared to be trapped inside but able to see out. The box hung heavy over the female figure. If it were to fall or be lowered, she would be crushed.

I was blown away by this physical representation that so closely resembled my dream. I never imagined I would see an image of what my glass elevator looked like, nor had I considered that such an image could be created in the material world. I was awestruck that this image existed in someone else's mind.

I took out my notebook and wrote: "Everything in this image is fragile, just as in my dream. Me, the glass, the elevator, the suspension." I asked the voices about the enormous explosion of atoms and cells in my dream.

The explosion is the work of Spirit-God-energy to dissolve old structures so that things can be made new.

"And was 'new' made within me in July 1991, twenty years ago this month? I do not understand what this change was in me. Was the elevator the beginning of the end of my political work? After the dream, we passed legislation, and Clinton and Gore were elected. Clinton extended the moratorium until the international treaty was signed. Was Gore's nomination as vice president a signal that all this would transpire?"

Your work with Gore led him to support a test ban, which enabled him to support Clinton on the test ban. Being vice president was an even greater launching pad for Gore's environmental work, which is directly connected to the work of the people: all of you who wish to preserve the planet for posterity.

"This piece of art appears to be a lament for men in their metal and mental buildings, who don't touch the earth. It's a lament for all of us, including the woman with an enormous weight above her that could crush her at any moment, and the men in their suits, lonely, separate from each other, looking out. Inside the structure, a piece of plastic, folded like a maze, seems to be the elevator. A maze! Can we find our way out?"

And then I saw that Hendrix's artwork could also represent us three—Al and Aaron trapped inside the structure of government, and me underneath, representing all those outside of government crushed by the weight.

You—and everyone else—are of course crushed by the weight of the nuclear arms race. It hangs heavy over your head: the men's mental work, the quest for power, the idiocy and stupidity of building nuclear weapons and nuclear reactors. The trillions of dollars spent on an artificial defense. You are crushed by all the mental activity and the patterns of racism and sexism that drive the fear and insanity. It is the crush of what was and is happening in the world. You know it. You knew it then. You saw it happening. It's why you did the work. It's why you are writing this book.

The number of nuclear weapons between the U.S. and Russia has been reduced to one-third their former size. This reduction is a great step forward for humanity, but it is not nearly enough.

Stay the course. Every effort in this direction is a boon to all of humanity.

"I see that the explosion was about transformation. It was a blaze of light to illumine the course of human events."

Such explosions, great and small, occur whenever anyone decides to make the world a better place.

Epilog

In the 1980s and 1990s, millions of people in the U.S., Europe, Australia, New Zealand, Japan, the South Pacific, and the Soviet Union worked to reduce the nuclear threat and halt the devastation caused by radiation leaked onto land and into groundwater and vented into the atmosphere. People signed petitions and wrote letters; organized local coalitions; participated in nonviolent protests; committed civil disobedience; took photographs and interviewed victims of nuclear testing; researched and wrote papers and books; educated people about the effects of nuclear weapons testing and production and nuclear reactors; and worked to pass legislation in city councils, state legislatures, and parliaments. Every person and every action was important.

Today there are approximately 20,000 nuclear weapons between the U.S. and Russia, down from 60,000 in the early 1980s. It is a huge change, a huge victory, but it is not enough. Decaying nuclear reactors exist throughout the U.S. and in dozens of other countries. A handful of reactor meltdowns or nuclear bomb explosions would devastate entire cities or countries. A nuclear war could end life on Earth.

As well, the planet and its inhabitants are facing a crisis of tragic proportions. The daily news tells of droughts, floods, food and water crises, wars fought over access to drug routes and oil, melting glaciers, and economic collapse. To know just a few of the details can be overwhelming: Indian farmers committing suicide by the thousands after being coerced to plant genetically modified crops that subsequently failed; populations of whales and seals sunburned because of holes in the ozone; Iraqi women bearing babies with atrocious deformities as a result of depleted uranium and other radioactive substances used by U.S. forces in Iraq.

To know what my own country, the United States of America, is doing is shocking. Documented situations include providing guns to drug lords in Mexico through a program called Fast and Furious; holding over 2.5 million people in prisons without recourse, many of whom are immigrants (a higher percentage of the population in prison than in Russia, China, Iraq, or Iran); providing funds for Afghanistan to grow poppies destined to be sold as opium. Who knows what else?

The greed of multinational corporations has brought decades of environmental destruction and a gaping disparity between the wealthiest individuals and the rest of humanity. Climate change, spurred by carbon dioxide and other greenhouse gases, is destroying crops and creating suffering for billions of people worldwide. The impact has been enormous on rainforests, the oceans, watersheds and deltas, the world's food supply, polar bears, red-winged blackbirds, bats, bees, and more. In the U.S. alone, economic disparity threatens the lives and livelihoods of millions of seniors, veterans, students, the ill and disabled, single parents, small business owners, farmers, and those unemployed or under-employed.

At the same time that the world seems to be spinning out of control, a dramatic shift in personal awareness is also taking place. More and more people are opening to the understanding that we are one people with one destiny, that everything is made of the same energy, the same essence, and that we are interconnected in ways we never before dreamed were true. One only need visit a social media tool such as Twitter to become aware of the thousands of individuals offering themselves as spiritual teachers, coaches, and guides to a new awareness.

This blossoming in personal awareness, which has touched the lives of many, is crucial to the future of the planet, yet the weight and momentum of materialistic values, unconsciousness, and a feudal mentality continue to drive our planet ever closer to destruction. Some say it is too late to redirect the course of human events and alter the fate of the planet; others hold out hope that an epiphany in human consciousness will bring about a new day.

I believe that another way is needed, one that involves intention and willingness to act. It is apparent that we cannot reverse the current trends by doing things as they have always been done. Indeed, it is a grave understatement to say that the old ways have not worked; that what we are doing collectively as the world's people is not working now. There is an extreme necessity for a new way of being in the world.

This new way requires living and acting from a place of love. The approach may seem to be a radical one: Love unconditionally those whom you hate, those you don't understand, those you disagree with, and those who are doing you wrong. Included is everyone you complain about, fear, or despise: political leaders, heads of banks and corporations, members of the Jihad, other religious extremists, and anyone else who makes it onto your personal list. Love and kindness may seem irrelevant to the hard realities of politics and corporate greed. Yet this is not a naïve approach. Political change depends upon individual change, and individuals can change when they are listened to and related to from a place of love.

Unconditional love is a key concept of many religions and humanistic approaches. It is the central teaching of the person of Jesus. Although spiritual leaders of various traditions have taught and modeled unconditional love, the teachings are not reserved for a select few. One does not need to be a spiritual teacher or an enlightened being to flow love to the world.

Messages from God/Spirit are crucial to this endeavor, offering guidance for our personal fulfillment and the future of the planet. A few may hear a voice inside their heads, but for many the messages will come from a dream, a friend, a book, a sermon, or nature, reverberating like a bell of truth. If unheeded, the messages will express themselves through the body, manifesting in exhaustion, stomach or back pain, chronic fatigue, cancer, diabetes, or heart disease. Such messages may tell us to change our line of work, speak up about an issue that concerns us, or change our priorities for the sake of generations to come. Frightened by the thought of what may be required of them, many people reject the messages in favor of what is known and familiar. Some have rejected the clues for decades, inviting soul death and eventually physical death as well.

It is essential to the survival of humanity that we the people take our love, kindness, and compassion into the seats of power: government, politics, and the large corporations. As long as we fail to do so, our governments will fail to serve us. All of us—people, animals, nature, and the planet herself—will continue to suffer in a downward-reaching spiral. In order for increased consciousness to reverse this trend, we must allow ourselves to be led to take an empowered role in our shared fate, so that our increased awareness infuses and transforms our life in community.

Other elements crucial to this work are knowing ourselves as spiritual beings so that we act from our true nature; a willingness to see what is happening in the world; a commitment to act from a place of love in all situations, including those that seem most difficult and challenging; and a process for clearing our emotions in order to free our thinking and our ability to act on the basis of love.

Nonviolent social action is the clarion call of many social reformers, as it should be. Nonviolence has been shown to be more effective than violent action in making social change. In general, observers tend to empathize when the action is nonviolent, which is seldom the case when action turns violent. In acting without violence, we also model the world we seek to create, and we develop the awareness and skills needed to manage and live in that new world.

The love described herein goes beyond nonviolence to seek out and affirm the divine essence within each person. This is an active love, one that involves getting to know and attempting to understand "the other" as one's neighbor on our shared voyage on planet Earth. At this critical time, I believe that we need more than nonviolent action. It is essential that we go beyond nonviolence to an active love.

While most of the events described in this book occurred between 1982 and 1995, the need to understand the truth and power of active love is greater now than ever. Inspired by revolutions, civil uprisings, and major protests throughout North Africa and the Middle East, the Occupy Wall Street movement that began in New York City on September 17, 2011, has sprung up in over 1,700 towns and cities worldwide. The message of the Occupy movement, "We are the 99%," speaks for all those whose lives and whose planet have suffered at the hands of a few. In truth, they speak for the 100%.

The Occupy movement addresses a deeper need as well: the need to lead a meaningful life. Just as our planet and its inhabitants cry out for help, our souls cry out for meaning. What can be more meaningful than helping to set humanity and our Earth mother on a positive, life-sustaining course? Finding deeper meaning requires seeing clearly the state of the world and being willing to engage in solving the problems. First, we must ask the questions, *What is my role? What can I do to help?* It is a process of asking, listening, and acting, then stopping again to listen and to act. We must trust enough to take the first step, which often requires that we venture into new and unfamiliar territory. By taking the first step, we can know what steps to take next.

If we heed the guidance of our heart and the voice of Spirit, we find that our actions become increasingly more loving and nurturing of ourselves and others. We do not have to give up rich, fulfilling, pleasurable lives. On the contrary, acting in the world from a place of love creates and enhances such lives.

To preserve our planet for generations to come, we must take the energy of love into the corporate, medical, educational, political, environmental, religious, agricultural, and civic realms. Everyone is needed. Everyone must help.

I invite you to listen to your heart, body, and soul, and the voices of Spirit and Mother Earth—to listen, and then to act.

44 Ways Love Changes Things

Offered here are forty-four ideas for taking love, kindness, and compassion into your political, community, and family settings. I encourage you to try them out and share the ideas with others. You may think of other ideas. Have fun, and enjoy being the bearer of clarity and light!

A Prescription for Living

The following set of five steps, based on the work of Angeles Arrien, affirms my approach to spiritual-political work. A friend introduced me to Arrien's list of four steps (#1, 2, 3, and 5) during the years I worked in Washington, D.C. I have added #4, which I felt was crucial to its success. The five steps form a brilliant prescription for living, which I have followed for over twenty years. I heartily recommend it to others. The prescription is a powerful guide for how to "be" in situations ranging from family issues to relationships to social change. I encourage you to memorize the list, post a copy next to your telephone, and stash another in your wallet.

1. Show up (for whatever presents itself).

2. Listen carefully.

3. Tell the truth without blame.

4. Act on the basis of love, not fear.

5. Let go of outcomes.

6. Choose an issue you care deeply about. Resolve to make a difference on this issue.

7. Ask your own inner guidance and other people what you can do to help.

8. Look for the spiritual essence, the heart and soul, of every leader and relate to that essence with love and kindness in your heart.

9. Ask elected officials about their values, basic assumptions, hopes, and dreams, and listen to their answers.

10. Pray for a politician.

11. Take homemade cookies or a bowl of fruit to your congressional office or mayor's office and smile at everyone you encounter there. Do this without any expectations or personal agenda.

12. Thank every public servant you meet for taking on the job.

13. Treat elected officials the way you treat your friends.

14. Make friends with one public official, using the "Prescription for Living."

15. Send a thank you letter when you are pleased with someone's vote.

16. Call or write your senator, congressman/woman, mayor, state legislator, or school board representative about what matters to you. When an elected official receives 25 phone calls in a single day, they take note. Elected leaders also believe that every letter they receive represents at least 1,000 people who feel the same, but did not take the time to write. You are speaking for all those people.

17. Write your member of Congress on behalf of a child, older person, or disabled person.

18. Prior to an election, write a letter to the editor about the issues you care most about. Candidates for office will take note.

19. Write a letter to the editor to appreciate things your mayor is doing to help the community.

20. Before writing or calling, feel love in your heart. If this is difficult, think of the other person's spiritual essence or soul. Feel love for this soul.

21. When you are angry, despairing, or afraid because of the actions of political leaders or because of the tasks you are considering doing, sit in silence to experience and observe your feelings. Whenever possible, do this before you act. (See "Presence Practice" in the resource list at end of the book.)

22. Be grateful for being able to vote. Think of all the people in the world who do not have a say in the governance of their country.

23. Vote. If you feel discouraged about politics, vote anyway. Write in the name of a candidate if you do not think the other candidates represent your values.

24. Notice when laws are passed that support human life, animal life, or the planet, and tell a friend or group of friends. Spread the good news.

25. Call on a higher power to guide our country.

In Meetings

26. In small group meetings, request that everyone be allowed to speak once before anyone speaks twice.

27. If women, people of color, young people, or any other constituency is not being heard, make a point of listening and ask the rest of the group to do likewise.

28. Encourage quiet people to speak. Encourage loud people to listen.

In Your Community

29. Seek opportunities to talk to people of different races, nationalities, and life experiences. Listen to what they have to say.

30. Listen to a child, an older person, or a disabled person.

31. If you are a white person, listen to a person of color talk about their life.

32. Write a letter to the editor about your hopes and dreams for your community and your country.

33. Thank those who participate in trying to solve a problem.

34. In a conflict situation, look for even small points you can agree on.

35. Ask yourself, "Who do I think is the enemy? People on the right or left? My elected officials? The CEO of a corporation? A police officer? A group of anarchists?" Try to take their point of view. If you appreciate some aspect of their behavior or if you can understand some aspect of what motivates them, use this as the basis of a conversation.

36. Pick up trash on your city or neighborhood streets.

37. Leave your picnic area or hiking trail cleaner than when you arrived.

<u>In Your Family</u>

38. Make a list of the values you hold most dear. Post it for friends and family to see. Invite them to make their own list.

39. Praise your children when they speak the truth. Do not punish them when they don't. Try to understand why they felt they couldn't tell the truth.

40. Teach your children (or somebody else's) about teamwork.

41. Take your children on a walk to pick up trash. Invite your neighbors to join you.

<u>Within Yourself</u>

42. Believe change is possible. Prove it to yourself by making a change.

43. Clear your emotions by using an emotional clearing process such as those listed in the resource section, writing, or simply by talking about them to a trusted friend.

44. Trust your own thinking and trust your own heart.

This list is a beginning. I welcome your ideas for how love can change things—ideas that could be added to the list. I also invite your questions about using this approach. I would love to hear your stories of taking love, kindness, and compassion into difficult places. Email me at carolinecottom@gmail.com.

Resources for Spiritual and Emotional Growth

1. *The Isle of Is: A Guide to Awakening,* book plus CD, by Caroline Cottom, Ph.D., and Thom Cronkhite, charts a journey of discovery in which you are the main character in the story of your own awakening. Throughout the journey, Spirit, nature, and your intuition lead you ever deeper into a place of peace, love, and connection to all things—the experience of awakening to who and what you really are. It's a "doing" book that includes guided meditations and energy experiences on the CD. Available from the authors at carolinecottom@gmail.com or at Amazon.com.

2. "The Journey" process for emotional clearing and healing was developed by Australian Brandon Bays. Workshops, CDs, and a book by the same name are available through her web site, www.thejourney.org. The home office is located at Journey Seminars Ltd, PO Box 2, Cowbridge, CF71 7WN, UK. Email: infoeurope@thejourney.com. Tel: +44 (0)1656 890 400.

3. "A Prescription for Living" comes from the work of Angeles Arrien, to whom the author is deeply indebted. Arrien's original work described four steps (steps #1, 2, 3, and 5 of the five-part "Prescription for Living"). She has since developed her four points into the Four-Fold Way® training program. See her web site: www.angelesarrien. com or contact her at P.O. Box 2077, Sausalito, CA, 94966, USA. Tel: (415) 331-5050.

4. "Presence Practice," described in *The Isle of Is: A Guide to Awakening* and guided on the CD included with the book, is based on ancient Indian practices. These practices were also transformed into the WaveWork® by Sandra Scherer, described below. Presence Practice provides a daily, moment-to-moment practice for releasing tension and increasing peace and joy in one's life. Both Presence Practice and the WaveWork® allow you to gently and deeply release painful emotion, as well as bring healing to areas of physical pain. Thom Cronkhite and Caroline Cottom teach Presence Practice at their workshops and spiritual retreats in the U.S. and Mexico. Visit their web site at www.sacred-messages. com or email Caroline at carolinecottom@gmail.com.

5. "Reaching Out," a ten-part PBS television series hosted by Ram Dass (aka Richard Alpert, Ph.D.), explores compassion and social change. For information about the series, go to www.reachingout.org or email mail@reachingout.org. Their offices are located at 6116 Merced Avenue #165, Oakland, CA 94611, USA. Tel: 510-665-6545.

6. Re-evaluation Counseling, also known as RC or co-counseling, is an emotional clearing tool taught in classes for use by pairs of co-counselors. RC enables co-counselors to live their lives more fully and to become effective at world change. Headquarters for The Re-evaluation Counseling Communities is located at 719 Second Avenue North, Seattle, WA 98109, USA. Email: ircc@rc.org. Web site: www.rc.org. Tel: 001-206-284-0311.

7. "Sacred Messages: Honoring the Infinite Self," is the author's blog of short articles and beautiful photographs designed to support readers in living from a place of love and peace. www.sacred-messages.com

8. The WaveWork® is an emotional healing process developed by Sandra Scherer (Dayashakti) during a twenty-year residency at Kripalu Center for Yoga and Health in Lenox, Massachusetts, USA. For more information, see www.thewavework.com or email waveworkfellowship@ earthlink.net.

The Many Gifts

A lightning bolt on a sweltery summer day.

A brilliant man from a neighboring district, destined to be a political star.

The one who ran his office, who understood and gave space for all that occurred.

The one who knew defense, whose complexity and depth hid behind a wall of distrust.

The love we found among us.

Dreams that persisted, insisted, resisted my turning away.

A dream life laid down for me, gifting me with a life lived in two worlds at once.

That Spirit gave me such a role.

Re-evaluation Counseling, which taught me to listen, ask the right questions, clear my emotions, and build relationships as a way to make lasting change.

Voices that led me, loved me, showed me the way.

The voice of Spirit, the only Spirit, the true Spirit, that lives in the ever-present.

The voice that came through Phyliss to guide me through the wilderness.

Louise and Linda, companions on my journey to a new way of being.

My family—Ron, David, and Amy—who stayed at my side as I

followed the voice of Spirit into the halls of Congress and to the heart of the earth.

A world that hears and feels love and alters its course.

Thom, who has shown me to a life lived fully in Spirit.

All of this, and more.

I take it all as a gift.